Chasing

the Wild Goose

The Story of the Iona Community

Ronald Ferguson

Ronald Ferguson is Minister of St Magnus Cathedral in Kirkwall, Orkney.
After seven years in journalism, he studied at St Andrews University, graduating MA with honours in History and Philosophy, and at New College, Edinburgh, graduating BD with first class honours in New Testament studies. A postgraduate year at Duke University, where he was awarded the degree of Master of Theology, was followed by eight years' ministry in the Glasgow housing scheme of Easterhouse. After an exchange year with the United Church of Canada, he was deputy warden of Iona Abbey from 1980-81, and then elected Leader of the Iona Community from 1981-88.

He is the author of *Geoff: a Life of the Revd Geoffrey M. Shaw*; *Grace and Dysentery: Personal Reflections on a Visit to India*; *George MacLeod*, a much acclaimed biography of the founder of the Iona Community, *Black Diamonds and the Blue Brazil*, a 'cult' appraisal of his home town, Cowdenbeath in Fife, and its football team; *Technology at the Crossroads*; and two works for the stage 'Every Blessed Thing' and 'ORKNEYINGA'. He is also editor of *Daily Readings with George MacLeod*; joint editor of *The Whole Earth Shall Cry Glory: Iona Prayers* by the Revd George F. MacLeod. Ronald Ferguson has had short fiction and poetry published in the Glasgow *Herald*, for which he is a regular columnist

Contents

Preface to the Revised Edition

The Iona Community is immensely grateful to Ron Ferguson for his ready agreement to the publication of an extended version of *Chasing the Wild Goose*. The need and demand for an accessible account of the Iona Community's story is as strong as ever; and it is especially appropriate that I should be writing this at the time of the celebrations to mark the fourteen hundredth anniversary of St Columba's death and that this book should be published in the year of the Community's sixtieth anniversary.

Only minimal adjustments have been made to the text of the 1988 edition. The final chapter attempts to identify and explore the events and developments in the Community's life over the last ten years.

Royalties from this new edition will go to the Wild Goose Resource Group, a project of the Iona Community promoting and exploring new approaches to worship throughout Britain and beyond.

My personal thanks and warm appreciation go to all those who have helped assemble the additional material: as a former civil servant I recognize that my style can scarcely match that of an ex-journalist! I hope nonetheless that this book will continue to provide enrichment, stimulation, and perhaps challenge too, for all those who are interested in the work and concerns of the Iona Community.

Norman Shanks
Leader, Iona Community
Iona, Columba's Day, 1997

Bird of Heaven

Catch the bird of heaven,
Lock him in a cage of gold;
Look again tomorrow,
And he will be gone.

Ah! the bird of heaven!
Follow where the bird has gone;
Ah! the bird of heaven!
Keep on travelling on.

Lock him in religion.
Gold and frankincense and myrrh
Carry to his prison,
But he will be gone.

Temple made of marble,
Beak and feather made of gold,
All the bells are ringing,
But the bird has gone.

Bell and book and candle,
Cannot hold him any more,
For the bird is flying
As he did before

Ah! the bird of heaven!
Follow where the bird has gone;
If you want to find him,
Keep on travelling on.

Sydney Carter

Acknowledgements in the Revised Edition

I am grateful to Oxford University Press for permission to quote from *Adomnan's Life of St Columba* (A.O. and M.O. Anderson, 1961), and also for permission to quote from *The Letters of John Keats* (ed. M. Buxton Forman, 1952); to Colin Morton for permission to quote from Ralph Morton's book *The Iona Community: Personal Impressions of the Early Years* (Saint Andrew Press, 1974), and to Iona Community Wild Goose Publications and Wild Goose Resource Group for permission to quote various materials. The biblical extracts are from the Revised Standard Version, published by the American Council of Churches. The song 'Bird of Heaven' is reproduced by permission of Sydney Carter © 1969 Stainer and Bell Ltd from 'Green Print for Song'. Patrick Kavanagh's poem 'Beyond The Headlines' is reproduced by kind permission of the Trustees of the Estate of Patrick Kavanagh, c/o Peter Fallon, Literary Agent, Loughcrew, Oldcastle, Co. Meath, Ireland. The texts of the *Carmina Gadelica* were re-published in 1992 by Floris Books, Edinburgh

Acknowledgements in the Original Edition

There has long been a need for a book which tells the story of the Iona Community and describes its present-day life and work — and sets it within the context of Iona's remarkable history.

One way to tell the story would have been through the testimony of those who have been affected by the work of the Community on island and mainland, but this would have meant a multi-volumed work.

Some names are given here, but I am keenly aware of the many who could, or even should, have been mentioned. The full and detailed story must await a definitive academic treatise. I am grateful to those who read the first draft of the manuscript and made suggestions; at the end of the day the judgements are mine.

In the interests of narrative flow in what is intended as a popular yet well-grounded history, it was decided not to clutter the text with annotations. The quotations from the Iona Community history are from the Community's magazine, *Coracle*, unless otherwise stated. Those interested in pursuing historical researches further will find a selected bibliography at the end of the book.

All royalties from this book will go towards the work of the Iona Community.

I would like to record my thanks to the Council of the Iona Community for setting aside the necessary time for me to research and write the book in the course of a very busy and demanding year, and to the staff of the Community for their support and encouragement Thanks also to Offline Services, Edinburgh whose donation of a word processor made the compiling of the manuscript at first a terror and then a delight. My editors at Collins have been encouraging and enthusiastic.

I am grateful to George MacLeod, not only for kindly agreeing to write the foreword but also for his warm personal support. and to my wife, Cristine, for gently coping with writer's dementia.

The living story of the Iona Community continues. Today, Lord MacLeod laid the foundation stone of a new international youth centre on Iona, ensuring that future generations will have the opportunity to participate in a new stage of the divine chase — finding in the process that their lives are strangely changed.

Ron Ferguson
Leader, Iona Community
Iona, Columba's Day, 1987

Original Foreword
by the Very Revd Lord MacLeod of Fuinary,
Founder of the Iona Community

Here is a book our modern Church badly needs. Written by one who first trained as a journalist and later became a minister, it has both clarity and brevity and is marked by historical and theological excellence.

How many Christians are aware that Rome was not in charge of all Europe in the early centuries? On the contrary, the Celtic Church had a different date for Easter and an outlook of its own.

Coming up-to-date, how many know that the Church of Scotland is in the forefront of Church Unity — with Roman Catholic bishops conferring and worshipping with Presbyterians in Iona Abbey, and Roman Catholic bishops inviting Presbyterian Moderators to come to worship with them on that same site?

Iona is a congenial site for this and for so much more. It was Columba, on his deathbed, who anticipated that his monastery would one day be deserted but 'ere the world come to an end, Iona would be as it was'.

It is by this rebirth, now occurring in modern terms, that the membership of the Iona Community today is composed of Roman Catholics as well as Protestants, women as well as men — numbering some two hundred Members. Another eight hundred Associates are scattered across the world, and more than two thousand 'Friends' help with our finances. Nor is the Community any longer only concerned with clergy, male or female.

In the restored Abbey we put up fifty visitors a week who come to attend our conferences from March to October Two years ago we embarked on a scheme for further permanent buildings to hold an extra fifty a week, and so far three-quarters of the sum needed has come our way from thousands of donors — proof, surely, of God's concern for our purpose.

What Is Our Overall Purpose?

In a sentence, it is actually to apply on weekdays what we sing about on Sundays.

What Is The Matter?

That is the question that the Western world is everywhere asking, both in the Church — with its lessening numbers in all denominations — and in the world, with its ever more ominous nuclear confrontation.

The short answer is that 'Matter is the matter'.

About a hundred years ago the Church decided to concentrate on the spiritual and thereby left the weekday to science. After every Sunday benediction, on leaving the church the serious Christian pauses at 'the West Door' before returning to the world. And there is no 'West Door' as helpful as the West Door of Iona Abbey. Standing there, you are confronted by three crosses, two belonging to the tenth century and the third not much later.

St John's Cross is the first to get you back to the Truth. The opening chapter of his Gospel reads, 'The world was made through Christ *and without Him was not any thing made that was made*. In Him was Life and the Life was the Light of Men.' This means that Christ was and is *Creator* and not just Redeemer. Jesus, here and now, is as much involved in politics as He is in prayer. He is to be obeyed in material problems.

St Martin's Cross. Martin was a Roman who was born a pagan. He joined the army and the chaplain converted him to Christianity. He resigned and became a monk. Martin was horrified that the monks were only interested in their own salvation. He persuaded them instead to get back to comforting people in the towns, in the matters of their housing, their education and their employment. One of his fellow monks was an uncle of St Columba, and he went to Iona and showed Columba the kind of 'all-in' Christianity that so rapidly converted the West of Scotland.

St Matthew's Cross. Matthew was a tax gatherer. Such were even more loathed in his day than they are in ours. The love of money was the curse of Gospel times, as it is of ours today. In 1916, in Russia, revolutionaries (later to be known as Communists) rose in revolt against the Tsar of Russia. There were strong signs of the Tsar defeating and obliterating the Communists, but the money boys in France and Britain did not like him, so they gave millions of francs and millions of pounds to the Communists. This allowed the Communists to beat the Tsar!

How many people today know that it was European financiers who put the Communists on their feet for eighty years!

Our 'money boys' who did that were not rogues. Most of them 'went to church on Sundays', but thought the Gospel had 'nothing to do with moneymaking'.

I would ask the reader of this book — are you, as a person, careless of how you spend your money? Are you a moneylender like Matthew? Is his conversion not a challenge to you when you face his Cross outside your 'West Door'?

This book is about a faith for weekdays and not just Sundays.

Prologue

They come in their thousands every year from all over the world, clutching guide books and poly bags. They are church leaders and unemployed teenagers, theologians and workers, tourists and pilgrims and sceptics. They bring with them experiences, questions, problems and, most of all, yearnings. Might there be, in this ancient place of power and pilgrimage, a word from the Lord — or even just a word?

Iona is a small, rocky island in the Scottish Hebrides. Three and a half miles long and a mile and a half broad, it is not imposing. Why is it a magnet for so many people today? Why do they come, in fulfilment of St Columba's prophecy that to this small island homage will be paid by rulers and commoners?

Some come because of its history — tempestuous, bloody, thrilling and profoundly significant. They come to capture the spirit of St Columba and of the Celtic Church. They come to the ancient burial ground of Scottish and Norwegian kings, asking where the graves of Duncan and Macbeth can be found. They are drawn by the medieval abbey, hoping to recapture the chants of Benedictine monks, picturing them at prayer or working in the fields. Or they are following in the footsteps of the likes of Boswell, Johnson, Keats, Scott, Mendelssohn, Wordsworth, Robert Louis Stevenson, Prince Albert.

Others seek the fabled beauty of Iona — a Hebridean jewel in the Atlantic: the changing colours of the dancing sea, the whiteness of the sand and the quietness, the quietness.

The peace of Iona whispers to many. Iona has been described as 'a thin place', only a tissue paper separating the material from the spiritual. Many people have tried to express the experience — and have come back again and again.

Some come in search of healing, as many before them have done, dragging with them the physical ailments or emotional disorder of their lives, looking for a healing word or new courage to bear the pain. Still more come drawn by the work of the present-day ecumenical Iona Community which, after having rebuilt the living quarters of the Abbey, seeks to live the Gospel of justice and reconciliation in today's troubled world.

Yes, and many are tourists, clutching souvenirs, unsure whether to scoff or to pray. Among them are the post-Christian children of a fragmented and disquieted era. They are rightly suspicious of Celtic romanticism, medieval nostalgia, authoritarian clerics and trendy priests. They know there are things not right with the world they live in, not right with their own lives, but they are pretty sure that the old faith is as redundant as they often feel themselves to be. Pretty sure . . . Yet their feet have travelled this well-worn pilgrim way, walking with uneasy detachment. The feelings become even more mixed as the words spoken at the ancient shrine of piety turn out to be not just historical words, but contemporary syllables.

Today's pilgrim knows that many of the old bearings have gone. This is the age of baptized doubt. The age of faith and the age of reason are past, now it is the era of humanity come-of-age, post-Christian people with a question mark where their soul used to be. The experience of pilgrimage today can feel like following a traveller who walks in an eerie silence broken only by the tapping of his own white stick.

A Celtic symbol for the Holy Spirit is the Wild Goose, a turbulent sign which is more appropriate to living the faith in our day than is the gentle dove We live on a rollercoaster.

The story of the present-day Iona Community, which is the main theme of this book, represents one contemporary attempt to listen for the beating of wings This diverse community is composed of Protestants and Roman Catholics, ordained and lay, men and women, young and old, married and celibate. It is not a religious order in the conventional sense, yet it is bound together by a Rule of private prayer, economic sharing, and work for justice and peace. Its spiritual home is Iona, yet it lives mainly in dispersion in different parts of the world. Its staff are to be found in various locations — one, at the time of writing, in prison in protest against the arms race. Its oldest member and founder has been to New York on a speaking tour at the age of ninety-one, honoured there in the name of the world Church. And many people in different parts of the world are contributing towards the building of a new centre on the island, which will cater for young people well into the next century. It is not an easy community to categorize.

To understand its purpose we will have to travel to Glasgow in the 1930s; to understand its name and historical inspiration we must first journey to Iona from Ireland in the company of an Irish prince with blood on his hands, one who is called a saint.

Part One

THE BEATING
OF WINGS

1

The Dove of the Church

Columba's voyage from Ireland to Iona in AD 563 is one of the great foundational journeys of Western Christianity. The power of the man and the influence of his achievements can be gauged by the number of legends which surround him.

Getting access to the historical Columba is not easy. The written sources have to be handled with care — the writers were concerned not so much to record objective history as to provide inspiration for the faithful — but through the Dark Ages fog, however, the lineaments of a charismatic personality emerge. Before his birth in Donegal in 521, his mother, Eithne, is said to have been told by an angel in a dream that her son would be a prophet who would lead innumerable souls to the heavenly country. He was baptized Colum (Latin, *Columba*, which means dove).

The child's father, Phelim MacFergus, was a king or chieftain of the Uí Néill, descendants of the famed Niall of the Nine Hostages, who reigned in Ireland at the time of St Patrick. Colum's royal pedigree meant that he would have been a candidate for the High Kingship of Ireland, had his life not taken a different course.

Columba was fostered, as was the custom of the time, by a local priest. Adomnan, an abbot of Iona who wrote a life of Columba about a hundred years after the saint's death, tells how the priest one day observed his house covered in a bright light and saw a ball of fire over the face of the sleeping boy. The priest prostrated himself, interpreting the fire as a sign of the Holy Spirit. As a child, Columba was noted for the time he spent in church, and his boyhood nickname 'Columcille' (Dove of the Church) stayed with him till the end of his life.

The spread of Christianity in Ireland, ever since the inspired leadership of St Patrick in the fourth century, had been accompanied by the emergence of monastic schools as important places of learning and piety. As soon as he was old enough, Columba was sent to the monastic school of Moville headed by St Finbar, a noted scholar and traveller. At the end of his study Columba was ordained a deacon. He then moved south to Leinster, where he studied the literature and myths of old Ireland under the tutorship of Gemmen, a Christian bard, finding scope for the love of poetry and rhetoric which marked his style of expression.

A story from his time at Leinster is narrated by Adomnan. When Gemmen and Columba were studying in the open air, a girl ran towards them pursued by a man who caught her and stabbed her to death. Columba, who had tried to protect the girl, cursed the murderer who 'fell dead as did Ananias at the feet of St Peter'. It was the first of many powerful word-happenings attributed to Columba.

The youth's studies were completed at Clonard, the most famous seat of learning in all Ireland. Each student had his own wattle hut, and each was expected to work in the fields. Under the leadership of St Finnian, the students memorized large parts of the scriptures as well as copying sacred manuscripts. Thus were the élite of the Irish church trained.

By this time an ordained priest, Columba, who was already recognized as a leader by his peers, embarked on his missionary task. He headed north into Ulster, his home territory, and established a number of centres of mission and learning. With prodigious drive and energy, he set about converting whole tribes. There are stories of contests with Druid leaders, symbolizing the struggle between Christianity and pagan religion for the soul of Ireland. Columba himself had great respect, and indeed love, for the ancient Druidic traditions and wisdom: what he wanted to do was baptize them and bring them under the lordship of Christ. The establishment of important Christian centres at places such as Derry and Durrow reveals the saint's organizational and administrative abilities, as well as his love of learning.

It was this love of learning that led to a decisive watershed in his life. It appears that Bishop Finbar of Moville had returned from pilgrimage to Rome with a copy of the Vulgate version of the gospels. Columba is said to have secretly copied the manuscript, and Finbar took the matter up before the king. Diarmaid's famous judgement, 'To every cow belongs her calf', meant that Columba had to give up the copied document. The tradition is that Columba persuaded his kinsmen to fight against the king, who lost three thousand men. The battle was later interpreted as a victory of Christianity over Druidism, and Columba's prayers were felt to be the decisive factor.

Not everyone saw it as a victory for Christianity. Columba was no diplomat, and his achievements had won him enemies as well as friends. At a hastily convened Synod, he was tried in his absence and excommunicated! The sentence was revoked, however, and Columba was enjoined to win as many souls for Christ as had been killed in the battle.

Tradition has it that the impetuous Columba then went into self-imposed exile with twelve followers: that he set sail for Scotland; that he and his men landed several times on the west coast of Scotland but carried on because they could look back and still see Ireland; and that they reached Iona and stayed there, satisfied that Ireland could not be seen.

The legend of the saint turning his back on his homeland, attractive though it may be, is unlikely to be true. Columba returned to Ireland many times. It is much more likely that the saint was responding to a call from his kinsfolk who had settled in Dál Riata. Yet it was an exile of a kind. The Irish tradition of exile was making a sacrificial journey for Christ's sake, corresponding to the interior journey of the soul. The seas were the motorways of the day, and coracles — sturdy hidebound boats — regularly plied their trade off the coasts of Ireland.

So it was that Columba and his twelve followers, mainly relatives, landed on Iona on the eve of Pentecost, 563. As Adomnan put it, 'In the forty-second year of his age Columba, resolving to seek a foreign country for the love of Christ, sailed from Scotia to Britain.' The wings of the Wild Goose were beating.

Columba established his Iona community on the east side of the island, off the west coast of Mull, roughly on the site on which the medieval abbey now stands. Iona was known simply as 'I', or Island, and it is still known in Gaelic as I-Colum-Cille. ('Iona' itself is a corruption of the Pictish 'Ioua'; by a curious coincidence, Iona means 'dove' in Hebrew.)

The brothers — sometimes referred to as Island Soldiers — would have had individual 'bee-hive' mud and wattle cells (not unlike an African bush village), and the church itself was made of oak. Other buildings would have included the hospitium (guest house), refectory, scriptorium, barns, stables, mill, smithy, carpenter's shop and kiln. The fire in the kitchen would have been blessed and never allowed to go out.

Columba's cell, excavated a few years ago, was on a mound with a commanding view of the Sound of Iona. He slept on bare rock with a stone for his pillow.

The monks, who wore tunics with hooded cowls of undyed wool, were divided into three groups. The Seniors conducted the daily services in the church, taught students and copied sacred manuscripts; the Working Brothers were the farmers, craftsmen and labourers; and the Juniors were novices undergoing training. Worship, work and learning were seen as part of the same tapestry.

Not far from Iona is an island called, in Gaelic, 'The Island of Women'. The legend is that Columba would allow no women — or female cattle — on Iona.

The reputation of the community on Iona grew quickly, and curious visitors and pilgrims flocked to the island. Hospitality was a sacred monastic obligation, and Adomnan reports how Columba cancelled a fast day to give hospitality to 'a certain troublesome guest'. He also recounts the saint's legendary ability to sense when a guest was about to arrive. For example,

> On a day when the tempest was fierce and the sea exceedingly boisterous, the saint gave orders, saying, 'Prepare the guest chamber quickly and draw water to wash the stranger's feet.' One of the brethren enquired, 'Who can cross the Sound safely on so perilous and stormy a day!' The saint made answer; 'The Almighty has given a calm evening in this tempest to a certain holy and excellent man who will arrive here among us before evening.' And lo! that same day the ship for which the brethren had sometime been looking out, arrived according to the saint's prediction and brought St Cainnech. The saint went down with his brethren to the landing place and received him with all honour and hospitality.

Hospitality was sacred, because Christ was in the stranger. The Gaelic Rune of Hospitality puts it thus:

I saw a stranger yestreen:
I put food in the eating place,
Drink in the drinking place,
Music in the listening place:
And in the sacred name of the Triune
He blessed myself and my house,
My cattle and my dear ones.
And the lark said in her song
Often, often, often
Goes the Christ in the stranger's guise.
Often, often, often
Goes the Christ in the stranger's guise.

But Columba had not ventured to Scotland just to establish a colony of heaven. He was a missionary. He and his barefoot monks (known as the Peregrini — the wanderers) went out into the highways and byways to preach the Gospel. Iona was strategically well placed as a base for mission.

Christianity was, of course, far from unknown in Scotland. The great St Ninian, from his base at Whithorn in the fourth century, had inspired important evangelistic movements. But the impetus had waned under the pressure of tribal wars, and some of the fragile Christian communities had disappeared.

Columba shared Ninian's pioneering spirit. To win over the Picts in neighbouring Alban, he set out to visit High King Brude, near Inverness. The visit was also of strategic importance — the establishment of friendly relations with Brude would secure the development of Iona and enable the Columban monks to move around more freely. The historic journey included a sail up Loch Ness and, apparently, a joust with the Loch Ness monster! Adomnan reports that Columba saw men burying someone who had been attacked by a monster which then turned on one of the monks.

Columba moved into action:

The blessed man raised his holy hand and invoking the name of God he formed the saving sign of the cross in the air and commanded the ferocious monster, saying, 'Thou shalt go no further nor touch the man! Go back at all speed!' At the voice of the saint the monster was terrified and rushed down the river.

Loch Ness Monster 0, Columba 1. The heathen were impressed.

The events in Inverness were no less miraculous, according to the saint's biographer, with scenes reminiscent of the contests between Moses and Pharaoh.

The not unbiased account indicates that Columba and his followers sang vespers outside Brude's palace. The Druids tried to drown them out, but Columba sent terror through them by singing the forty-sixth psalm in the thunderous voice for which he was renowned. The doors were locked against them, but the saint made the sign of the cross and they burst open.

> The saint and his companions then passed through the gates. And when the king learned what had occurred, he and his councillors were filled with alarm, and immediately setting out from the palace he advanced to meet with due respect the blessed man, whom he addressed in the most conciliating and respectful language. And ever after from that day, the king held this holy and reverend man in high honour as was due.

Amidst all the legendary elements and embellishments which surround him, Columba stands out as a genuinely heroic figure. Under his leadership, Iona inspired disciples to preach the Gospel in often dangerous circumstances. The monks from the mother house established many foundations, often named after the saint.

Columba's fabled healing powers drew people to Iona — his prayers were felt to be particularly potent. Adomnan observes:

> By invoking the name of Christ this man of admirable life healed the disorders of various sick persons. For either by his merely stretching out his holy hand, or by the sprinkling of the sick with water blessed by him, or by their touching even the hem of his cloak, or by their receiving his blessing on anything, as for instance on bread or salt and dipping it in the water, those who believed recovered their health.

He was not a man who went in for non-directive counselling. His rebukes to sinners could be heard over on Mull. Yet his spirit of forgiveness and compassion, especially for the poor, was well known.

His love for all creation was equally renowned, and in Gaelic folklore he is the patron saint of cattle.

The importance of Columba and the pre-eminence of Iona can be seen in an event which occurred eleven years after his arrival on the island. Conall, king of the Dalriad Scots, died. Dál Riata was a key part of the Columban mission; its political future needed to be secured, so the choice of successor was crucial. Two brothers, Eoghan and Aidan, were the main contenders. Among the Gaels, the Arch-Druid or chief religious leader had a key role in the choice. Columba was the obvious guide. Although he was a close friend of Eoghan, Columba chose his brother, having dreamed three times that an angel of the Lord had commanded him to pick Aidan. Columba consecrated Aidan king of the Scots at a ceremony on Iona — the first king in Britain ever to be so consecrated.

Many poems are attributed to Columba and they were used by his followers as blessings and as protections against evil. His reputation as a poet lives on in the Gaelic prayer for 'the tongue of Columba in my head, the eloquence of Columba in my speech'. Phrases such as 'Columba the Good' are common in Gaelic speech.

In May 597, Columba told his monks he felt his end was near. Adomnan gives a touching account of the saint's last hours on 9 June 597. He says that while Columba rested on the grassy knoll near his cell, his old white pony came to him, whinnying and uttering plaintive cries. When Diarmit wanted to drive it away, Columba forbade him, saying,

> Let it alone as it is fond of me. Let it pour out its bitter grief on my bosom . . . to this brute beast devoid of reason, the Creator Himself hath evidently in some way made it known that its master is about to leave it.

From a hill above the monastery, Columba raised his hands and uttered the famous prophecy:

> Unto this place, small and mean though it be, great homage shall yet be paid, not only by the kings and people of the Scots, but by the rulers of foreign and barbarous nations and their subjects. In great veneration, too, shall it be held by holy men of other churches.

The saint went into his hut to work on his Psalter manuscript. When he had written the tenth verse of Psalm 34, 'They that seek the Lord shall not want any good thing', he said that Baithne, his chosen successor, must write the rest. He gave Baithne his last message for the brethren:

> These, my children, are the last words I address to you. That ye have unfeigned charity among your selves and if you thus follow the example of the holy fathers, God, the comforter of the good, will be your helper. And I, abiding with Him, will intercede for you, and He will not only give you sufficient to supply the wants of this present life, but will also bestow on you the good and eternal rewards which are laid up for those that keep His commandments.

When the bell rang for the midnight office, says Adomnan, the monks found the saint lying before the altar. One of them raised his right hand for him to bless the community.

> An angelic radiance filled the church round him on every side, and there the venerable old man sent forth his spirit to heaven into the delight and joyance of Heaven's household.

After saying Matins, the brothers, chanting the Psalms of the Dead, carried the body of the saint back to his cell.

2

The Celtic Way

The year in which St Columba died, a stranger from far-off parts slipped into Canterbury to inaugurate a Christian order of a different kind.

St Augustine had been sent by Pope Gregory of Rome — the same Gregory who, years before in the slave market, had described the fair-haired boys from Yorkshire as 'Not Angles but Angels'. The Roman mission gradually established itself, attending to the conversion of parts of England. The Iona monks were representatives par excellence of the Celtic form of the faith, and Columba its greatest saint. The two systems worked peaceably towards the evangelization of the whole of Britain — until conflict and choice became inevitable.

No one knows how or when Christianity first came to Britain. Some scholars believe it was brought by Roman soldiers, others by traders; and there is the legend that Joseph of Arimathea brought the faith to Glastonbury. What is sure is that there was an established Christian presence in Britain by the third century.

In 409 the Roman legions were withdrawn from Britain, and the country was invaded by the Saxons. Christianity was almost wiped out, except in those western parts of the land where the Celts — European tribes who had crossed the Channel to Britain about four hundred years before Christ — maintained their independence. St Ninian had established his base at Whithorn at the end of the fourth century, and St Patrick began his missionary work in Ireland in the early part of the fifth century.

It was a time of turmoil on the continental mainland. The break-up of the Roman empire and the barbarian invasions caused problems for a Church which had increasingly based its forms of government on the Roman administrative model. A further radical disturbance was the influence of ideas and practices from the East, mysticism and monasticism in particular. The theology and observances of the ascetics of the Syrian and Egyptian deserts brought new choices for Christians. People could opt for an 'ordinary' life in the world, living the faith within the normal structures of human and political life, or could withdraw from everyday concerns and pursue their Christian vocation either as a solitary or as a member of an intentional community. This radical new alternative was obviously particularly attractive in a time of social upheaval.

The Eastern monastic tradition took hold among the Celts, many of whom were by this time living in the western parts of the country and in Ireland, linked by a common group of languages. From it emerged a very distinctive and dynamic form of Christian life and expression.

The faith of the Celtic Church was orthodox, and differed from the continental Church only in matters of emphasis. They would have had no difficulty in recognizing each other as fellow Catholic Christians. Where they differed was in priorities, style and organization. The Celtic Church inhabited a monastic ethos which shaped its life and gave it a different 'feel' from the mainstream continental Church.

The Roman administrative system was largely based on cities; in church terms, the bishop, with his seat in the city, was the dominant figure. In Ireland and western Scotland, with their pastoral economies, the monastery was the natural centre of ecclesiastical authority and the abbot was the important person. The monastic system was highly suited to the Celts with their families and tribes.

The period from the fifth to the seventh centuries produced such outstanding devotion, commitment and missionary work that it is known as the 'Age of the Saints'. The light which burned in these dark ages was outstanding. The development was enhanced by the flow of writing from the East: scriptures, writings of the Church Fathers, and penitential texts. Monks of the desert corresponded regularly with Christians in other centres, and new manuscripts and translations were greatly prized.

Pilgrimages and retreats were essential features of Celtic spirituality. The ascetic discipline of peregrinatio (wandering, or pilgrimage) was common and, as we have seen, exile was not primarily a form of banishment but a spiritual journey. It was known as 'seeking the place of one's resurrection'. It was a journey led by the Wild Goose.

The Celts were clear that it was a pilgrimage of the heart. An old Irish poem put it thus:

> To go to Rome
> Is much trouble, little profit;
> The King of Heaven, whom thou seekest there,
> Unless thou bring Him with thee, thou wilt not
> find.

Pilgrims often went to island retreats, or to live in caves. Voyages were important forms of peregrinatio: sometimes the coracle would *boat* be allowed to drift, to let it land where it might. There the pilgrims would set up a simple place for contemplative prayer.

In the monasteries, daily worship and private prayer were central. Along with them went a severe penitential system. Penitential practices from the East, such as standing up to one's neck in water while reciting the Psalter, were taken over by the Celtic community. Standing up to one's neck in the Nile on a warm day was one thing; doing the same in the Sound of Iona was something else! (In the 1980s Iona Abbey was heated by an experimental system which drew its warmth from the sea — a divine mystery to those who have ever bathed there.) Other penances included spending the night in a tomb with a corpse, or singing the Psalter with arms outstretched in the shape of a cross; one Clonard monk made seven hundred genuflections a day and became a cripple.

Three types of martyrdom were identified. White martyrdom was when a man separated from everything he loved for the sake of God. Green martyrdom occurred when he separated from his desires by fasting and labour. Red martyrdom occurred when he poured out his blood for Christ's sake.

The purpose of these disciplines was the pursuit of holiness: a single-minded concentration on seeking the will of God. Each monk had an anamchara — a soul friend — who guided him in matters of the spirit. The disciple confessed his sins to his anamchara, who helped his fellow pilgrim along the way of Christ with friendship and support. The role of the anamchara was not seen as a priestly function, but as an essential part of Christian fellowship and growth. A Gaelic saying observed, 'Anyone without a Soul Friend is a body without a head'.

Corporate worship, usually five times each day, was an integral part of the life of the monastic community. The Eucharist was held in reverence. Feet-washing was a regular feature of Celtic worship. The biblical scriptures were venerated, as is seen by the beautiful handwritten texts.

Although scholarship and intellectual rigour were highly regarded, Celtic theology was marked by its lack of speculation. It often used the name of the Trinity, Father, Son and Holy Spirit — but did not philosophize about it. Celtic theology emphasized the conflict at the heart of life and Christ's victory over the powers of evil was a recurrent theme. Creation was reverenced and Christ was described as 'the true Sun'.

Celtic pre-Christian religious thinking emphasized the spirit in every thing, and Celtic Christianity simply baptized this tendency. The nature of Celtic spirituality is best seen in the runes, poems and hymns which have come down to us. The great hymn attributed to St Columba runs as follows:

> Christ is the world's redeemer,
> The lover of the pure,
> The fount of heavenly wisdom,
> Our trust and hope secure;
> The armour of His soldiers,
> The Lord of earth and sky;
> Our health while we are living,
> Our life when we shall die.
>
> Christ hath our host surrounded
> With clouds of martyrs bright,
> Who wave their palms in triumph
> And fire us for the fight.
> Christ the red cross ascended
> To save a world undone,
> And, suffering for the sinful,
> Our full redemption won.

Down in the realm of darkness
He lay a captive bound,
But at the hour appointed
He rose, a Victor crowned;
And now to heaven ascended,
He sits upon the throne,
In glorious dominion
His Father's and His own.

Glory to God the Father,
The unbegotten One;
All honour be to Jesus,
His sole-begotten Son;
And to the Holy Spirit —
The perfect Trinity,
Let all the worlds give answer,
'Amen — so let it be'.

The Celtic runes and poems are beautiful. They speak of the presence of God in all of life and a profound spirituality linked to a deep reverence for the earth undergirds the poetry.

The 'Rune of the Peat Fire' indicates that the first layer of peat should be laid down in the name of the God of life, the second in the name of the God of peace, and the third in the name of the God of grace.

The Sacred Three
To save,
To shield,
To surround
The hearth.
The house,
The household,
This eve,
This night;
Oh, this eve,
This night,
And every night,
Each single night.

The 'Prayer of Columba' gives a flavour of the Celtic prayers:

> Almighty Father, Son and Holy Ghost,
> Eternal ever-blessed gracious God,
> To me, the least of saints, to me, allow
> That I may keep a door in Paradise:
> That I may keep even the smallest door,
> The furthest door, the darkest coldest door,
> The door that is least used, the stiffest door,
> If so it be but in thine house, O God!
> If so it be that I can see Thy Glory,
> Even afar, and hear Thy Voice, O God!
> And know that I am with Thee —
> Thee, O God.

The Irish monks did not despise their native culture. Heathen lore and stories were collected in the monasteries and written down. The lyrical aspirations of Celtic monasticism are encapsulated in a seventh-century poem full of spiritual sensuousness:

> I wish, O Son of God, O son of the living God,
> O ancient eternal king,
> For a hidden little hut in the wilderness,
> that it may be my dwelling.
> An all-grey lithe little lark to be by its side,
> A clear pool to wash away sins
> through the grace of the Holy Spirit,
> A southern aspect for warmth,
> a little brook across its floor,
> A choice land with many gracious gifts
> such as be good for every plant,
> A pleasant church, and with the linen altar cloth,
> a dwelling for God in heaven,
> Then, shining candles above the pure white
> scriptures —
> This is the husbandry I would take,
> I would choose, and I will not hide it;
> Fragrant leeks, hens, salmon, trout, bees,
> Raiment and food enough for me from
> the King of fair fame,
> And I to be sitting for a while
> praying to God in every place.

It is easy to see the attraction of the Celtic Church in its heroic age.

For a hundred years after Columba's death, the Iona mission continued to send out powerful thrusts — into England, across the North Sea, to the Low Countries, into the territory of Charlemagne and beyond. The history of the founding of the Church in the midst of the chaos on the continent contains the names of Columbanus and Boniface and many others whose Christianity looked to Ireland or Iona.

The Venerable Bede reports that when King Oswald came to the throne of Northumbria in 625, he sent to the 'Scottish authorities' on Iona for Christian support. Thus the Saxon kingdom of Northumbria was served by Celtic monks from Iona, based in daughter foundations such as the holy island of Lindisfarne.

The mission to the North of England was highly effective, thanks to the holiness and wisdom of Aidan. The first person to be sent from Iona was Corman, who came back complaining that the English were ungovernable. Aidan quietly suggested that Corman had been too severe and that a gentler approach might bear fruit. But who would do it? Like many a person who makes an innocent suggestion at a committee meeting, Aidan found himself with the job. Bishop Aidan did not choose York as his seat, as his predecessor had done, but based himself at Linsdisfarne. He lived very simply, and he and his monks won over the people by their prayer, poverty and care for the poor. Bede wrote:

> Aidan gave his clergy an inspiring example of self-discipline and continence, and the highest recommendation of his teaching was that he and his followers lived as they taught. He never sought or cared for worldly possessions and loved to give away to the poor whatever he received from wealthy folk. In town or country he travelled on foot, stopping to talk with anyone he met, high or low, pagan or Christian. All who walked with him were expected to meditate and read scripture. If invited to dine with the king, he took along a couple of clergy, ate sparingly and left as soon as possible. If wealthy people did wrong he wouldn't keep quiet out of respect or fear, but corrected them outspokenly.

This tribute to a Celtic bishop is all the more remarkable coming from the quill of a man who fervently took the Roman side in the clash with the Celtic order. Ostensibly the argument was about two issues — the monks' tonsure and the dating of Easter. Celtic Christians and Roman Christians celebrated Easter at different times, and this was an embarrassment in an island where the two orders had grown up together. The Celts and Romans had different ideas about monastic tonsure — but sane people do not usually shed blood about hairstyles. The underlying issue was that of authority.

What had happened was that while the Benedictine form of Christian organization was directly under the authority of the Pope, Celtic Christianity, though entirely orthodox, had developed its own distinctive style, untouched by continental influences. New arrangements for the dating of Easter and styles of tonsure had bypassed the Irish and Scots, who were the conservatives in the matter.

The issue came to a crisis when King Oswiu of Northumberland, brother and successor of Oswald, married a daughter of King Edwin, who came under the Roman obedience. This meant that the king celebrated Easter while his queen fasted.

Oswiu summoned the two parties to the Synod of Whitby in 663. Bishop Wilfrid, who spoke for the Roman obedience, accused the Celts of arguing that the whole world was wrong except them. Bishop Colman of Lindisfarne advocated the Celtic dating of Easter and the tonsure.

In his historic judgement, King Oswiu came down in favour of the Roman party. The decision had little practical effect at first. The Celtic Church, by and large, simply carried on as before, but its position and influence were undermined. In 718 Iona celebrated Easter according to the Roman dating. Iona's pre-eminence gave way to the priority of Dunkeld in Scotland and Armagh in Ireland. Why did the Celtic Church lose the battle? The answer lies in its lack of a cohesive organization. The loose structure centred on tribes and families, held together by monastic links, was simply not strong enough.

The Iona monks faced another external threat at the beginning of the ninth century, when longships started to appear on the horizon. The Viking visitors had not come on pilgrimage. The monastery was plundered, then sacked, and in 806 the blood of sixty-eight monks poured into the white sands of what is now known as Martyrs Bay. They had made their red martyrdom.

The community decided to go to Ireland and a new base was established at Kells. Columba's remains were taken over there, along with, some scholars believe, an illuminated manuscript now famous as the Book of Kells. The saint's relics were brought back to Iona in 818; seven years later the monk Blathmac, the principal member of the community on the island, was slaughtered by Norse raiders for refusing to reveal their hiding place. The remains were taken back again to Ireland in 831 and are believed to be buried at Downpatrick, along with St Patrick and St Brigid. A little chapel, St Columba's Shrine, is built over the saint's last resting place on Iona.

To withstand the Norse threat, it was necessary for the Picts and the Scots to unite. Kenneth MacAlpine, of the blood of Columba's clan and King of the Scots, claimed the Pictish throne and effected a united kingdom in 844. This great step towards the forging of a Scottish nation owed not a little to Columba's historic role in securing the kingdom of Dál Riata. Kenneth rebuilt the church at Dunkeld, near the royal capital of Scone, and took some of Columba's relics there. It was appropriate that this king, descended from the man Columba had consecrated on Iona, should have installed symbols of the saint's power in the heart of the royal church.

Although Dunkeld — well inland and therefore protected from the Vikings — was now the centre of Scottish ecclesiastical authority, Iona was revered as holy ground. Kenneth MacAlpine was buried in the Reilig Oran, the island graveyard, in 860. It is believed that forty-eight Scottish kings, including perhaps Duncan and Macbeth, eight Norwegian kings, and a number of Irish and French monarchs lie in the ancient graveyard, which still serves as the island burial place. The bodies of the kings were brought over from the island of Inchkenneth, and borne along the Street of the Dead (which was excavated in the 1950s).

The kings wanted to be buried there for two reasons. Firstly, when the Last Trump sounded and the dead rose from their graves to face the Judgement, it might be possible to hang on to the coat-tails of a saint, and some of the Scottish kings would need all the help they could get. Secondly, Columba was believed to have prophesied that when the world came to an end, the whole earth would be covered by water, except Iona. How much better to rise dry! (There is an old Gaelic prophecy to the effect that Christ's Second Coming will take place on Iona.)

It is from the tenth century that the magnificent stone standing crosses of Iona date. St Martin's Cross is typical of the Irish standing crosses, with the west face carved with scenes from the Bible and the east face containing a fine example of Irish artistic sculpture — the intertwining lines signifying the indissolubility of life now and hereafter. The circle round the cross, so characteristic of Irish crosses, is believed to be borrowed from the circle of laurel leaves placed on the head of the victor of the Roman games — thus changing the cross of defeat into the cross of victory. St Martin, to whom the cross is dedicated, was a fourth-century Roman soldier who became a Christian and founded a monastery in the south of France. He influenced Ninian and the pioneers of the Age of the Saints. The stump of St Matthew's Cross is all that remains; and St John's Cross, which stands outside St Columba's shrine, is a reinforced concrete replica of the original, which was badly damaged in the Hebridean gales.

Columban monks continued to worship on Iona. The office of abbot had been succeeded by that of the Coarb of Columcille (heir of Columba), who usually ruled the community from Ireland. In the eleventh century, the Western Isles fell into the hands of Malcolm Canmore, son of Duncan and successor to Macbeth on the Scottish throne. His wife Margaret, a Saxon princess who brought her English ways and speech into the Scottish court, was a devout member of the Roman Church. She is said to have rebuilt some of the Iona monastery and St Oran's chapel, the oldest ecclesiastical building still standing on the island. Queen Margaret was keen to Latinize the Church in Scotland, and her policies eventually led to the abolition of the Celtic liturgy and the strengthening of the Roman order. In 1093 the Western Isles were ceded to Magnus Barelegs, King of Norway, who made a pilgrimage to the island out of reverence for Columba.

But the fires of faith were burning low; the era of Celtic Christianity was well and truly over. Its dynamism and creativity, its art and sense of creation, its seeing God in all things, and its genuine heroism were profound contributions to the life of the Christian West. Despite all the romantic exaggerations, Celtic expressions of Christian faith, seen pre-eminently in the lives of its saints, remain winsome and attractive and not without relevance to today's world.

By the twelfth century, Columba's Iona children were a quarrelsome and dispirited group who had lost their way — symbolized by the island's continually changing political lordship. In 1156 came another change with important consequences. Somerled, Chieftain of Argyll, made his son Reginald Lord of the Isles. A new and significant chapter in the Iona story was about to begin. The Wild Goose was sighted in the sky again.

3

The Glory of the West

Or was it the gentle dove that reappeared?

To step inside the restored Benedictine Abbey on Iona is to experience strength, limits, order and peace. Structure — fine structure — and organization shaped the medieval expression of Christian faith and life.

In 1203, Reginald, Lord of the Isles, asked the Benedictine order to come to Iona and establish a new Iona community on the site of the Columban foundation. A stable, ordered community required a stable, ordered home, one made of stone. Gradually the Abbey buildings took shape in a rhythm of work and worship, worship and work. The accent was less on mission than on regular worship of the living God within the strong walls of a fine sanctuary, conducted within the ultimate framework of a cohesive, structured mother Church. Outside the walls of that Church, salvation was not possible.

We have left the world of Peregrini, pilgrimage and exile, and White, Green and Red martyrdom. There are fewer staring-eyed madmen about. There is less self-inflicted poverty and more contentment. Worship and common sense join hands. Security is more evident than adventure, and the boundaries of things are clear. Life is moderate and good, with priorities clearly laid down. The exciting, erratic heroes have gone, replaced by ordinary workaday saints.

The Benedictine monks brought new life to an Iona which needed renewal. As with the Celts, community was the matrix of Christian life. The island became again a powerhouse of prayer as the monks went about their daily business of worship, work, scholarship and hospitality. There was one incursion of Celtic clerics from Ireland, claiming Iona as their rightful inheritance, but generally the brotherhood lived free from outside interference, though directly under the jurisdiction of Rome. The community was under the direction of an abbot, assisted by a prior. Many of the monks came from Mull, and it was common for the powerful aristocratic Mull families to provide recruits.

The Mackinnons of Mull, descendants of Macbeth, provided several abbots of Iona. Abbot Finguine Mackinnon became notorious — accused of using Abbey property for his own ends and living with concubines. He was known as a conspiratorial figure in the political life of the Western Isles, and while he intrigued — he was eventually spared death only because he was an abbot — the Abbey buildings were neglected. Mackinnon's attempt to keep the abbacy in the family failed, and it passed instead to Dominic Mackenzie who, nervous of Mackinnon manoeuvres, beseeched the Pope to confirm his appointment right away, as 'the Abbey is situated in the isles among the wild Scots'.

Dominic set about making substantial repairs to the Abbey buildings, beginning about 1430, and the Abbey as we see it today belongs primarily to that time, although parts of it go back to the early thirteenth century.

Like all medieval abbeys, the building is a composite one. The first building was considerably smaller and narrower than the present one (evidence of the original church can still be seen) but under Dominic, the church was widened and lengthened, stretching almost to the end of the present sanctuary. The master mason was Donald Obrolchan, whose inscription is on one of the pillars. Donald, from a well-known family of Highland masons, carved scenes from the Bible and everyday life. On the arch above the crossing, directly facing the site of the medieval pulpit, the face of a soul in torment grimaces — a visual aid to remind the preacher of the fate of his hearers if he did not proclaim the message of salvation! On the south wall is the sedilia, where the celebrant sat during the Mass, and next to that the piscina, or sink, through which the water used for the ablutions drained into the earth outside. On either side of the south window are the figures of a monkey and a cat — the monkey symbolizing activity and the cat contemplation, the two aspects of the Christian life which the Benedictines held to be important. Instead of being a straightforward single-level church, it became split-level, with a raised sanctuary and a high altar (made of Iona marble) and a crypt below.

It is right that Abbot Mackenzie's effigy should lie in the sanctuary, but it is perhaps ironic that his recumbent partner should be John, the Mackinnon abbot who succeeded him. Lying at peace, Abbot John looks every inch the spiritual churchman. He is, however, more accurately known as a wily and worldly politician. John owed his position as abbot to the lay patron of the Abbey, the Earl of Ross. The patrons exercised considerable influence, threatening to withdraw wealth and relics as forms of blackmail. It was easy for the abbacy to become a political gift.

The forfeiture of the Lordship of the Isles meant the end of lay patronage and influence, and thus more direct ecclesiastical intervention. At the end of the fifteenth century, the Pope was asked to erect the Abbey into a cathedral church. He granted the abbacy to the Bishops of the Isles, who were allowed to use the Abbey, which became known as the Cathedral of St Mary, without themselves becoming Benedictines. Thus Iona Abbey, which had prided itself on its independence, was subsumed under local ecclesiastical authority.

While all the politicking went on, the monks went about their daily business of prayer and work, receiving guests whose lives were renewed and enriched. Iona's reputation as a spiritual centre continued, helped also by the Augustinian nuns whose house was situated to the south of the Abbey buildings. Founded in the thirteenth century, the nunnery has few records, and little is known about its work. In the early fifteenth century, one nun, the illegitimate daughter of an Iona priest, was granted dispensation to hold religious office. The nunnery buildings were rebuilt in the fifteenth century but fell into disrepair after the Reformation.

Although the Lordship of the Isles was no more, family rivalries continued. It was the turn of the Campbells and the Macleans to seek the abbacy and now the bishopric. The rivalry continued until the Reformation, when the Campbell-influenced Bishop of the Isles, John Carswell, was a Protestant sympathizer. He translated the Church of Scotland's *Book of Common Order* into Gaelic, thereby making the Protestant liturgy available in the vernacular.

At the Reformation the Iona monks were dispersed to places such as Ratisbon, Douai and Rome. (The nuns were left in peace until they died.) The Abbey buildings, no longer resounding to the chants of monks, fell into disrepair. Thus was fulfilled Columba's prophecy:

> Iona of my heart, Iona of my love,
> Instead of monks' voices, there shall be lowing of
> cattle.

For some time the Abbey was used for Protestant worship and then, at the beginning of the seventeenth century, King Charles I appointed a bishop to Iona, giving him a grant to repair part of the Abbey. The bishop, Neil Campbell, blocked off the nave and turned it into a T-shaped cathedral. Scotland, however, declared for Presbytery, not Episcopacy. Neil Campbell turned with the nation and moved to a church in Campbeltown, taking the abbey bells with him.

The Macleans held Iona for some years, but in 1691 the island was decisively won back by the Campbells, who appointed factors to administer Iona. The spiritual needs of the islanders, who varied in number from two hundred to over five hundred were looked after, somewhat ineffectively, by the Synod of Argyll.

The memory of Iona as a spiritual centre remained strong, and in the latter part of the eighteenth century visitors began to come, to linger in the ruins and meditate on past events. Two such visitors were Dr Samuel Johnson and his scribe, Boswell. Johnson commented that the inhabitants were gross and neglected. The high altar was in fragments and cows wandered around the ruins of the church. Local islanders used the stones from the Abbey to build their own byres and dykes.

Even in its state of dissolution, Iona moved Dr Johnson, who observed:

> That man is little to be envied whose patriotism would
> not gain force upon the plain of Marathon, or whose
> piety would not grow warmer among the ruins of Iona.

Another visitor was Sir Walter Scott, who described the inhabitants as being in the last state of poverty and wretchedness. He was distressed by the condition of the ruins, in view of the fact that 'from this rude and remote island the light of Christianity shone forth on Scotland and Ireland'.

Keats visited Iona in 1818 and wrote to his brother in London about Columba's achievements:

> This saint became the Dominic of the barbarian Christians of the north and was famed also far south — but more especially was reverenced by the Scots, the Picts, the Norwegians and the Irish. In the course of years the island was considered the most holy ground of the north.

The poet tells amusingly how the old schoolmaster on Iona showed him round the ruins; 'He stops at one glass of whisky unless you press another, and at the second unless you press a third.'

William Wordsworth wrote about landing on Iona:

> How sad a welcome! To each voyager
> Some ragged child holds up for sale a store
> Of wave-worn pebbles, pleading on the shore
> Where once came monk and nun with gentle stir
> Blessings to give, news ask, or suit prefer.
> Yet is yon neat trim church a grateful speck
> Of novelty amid the sacred wreck
> Strewn far and wide. Think, proud philosopher!
> Fallen though she be, this Glory of the West,
> Still on her sons the beams of mercy shine,
> And hopes, perhaps more heavenly bright than thine,
> A grace unsought and unpossest,
> A faith more fixed, a rapture more divine
> Shall gild their passage to eternal rest!

Returning from Iona, the poet wrote this farewell:

> Homeward we turn. Isle of Columba's Cell,
> Where Christian piety's soul-cheering spark
> (Kindled from Heaven between the light and dark of time)
> Shone like the morning star, farewell!

Wordsworth was followed by Felix Mendelssohn in 1828. When his sisters asked him to tell them something about the Hebrides, he commented, 'It cannot be told, only played'. He then seated himself at the piano and played the theme which grew into the 'Hebridean Overture'. The composer wrote from Glasgow:

> Iona, one of the Hebrides-sisters — there is truly a
> very Ossianic and sweetly sad sound about that name
> — when in some future time I shall sit in a madly
> crowded assembly with music and dancing round me,
> and the wish arises to retire into the loneliest
> loneliness, I shall think of Iona, with its ruins of a
> once magnificent cathedral, the remains of a convent,
> the graves of ancient Scottish kings and still more
> ancient northern pirate-princes — with their ships
> rudely carved on many a monumental stone.

Prince Albert (while Queen Victoria remained on the royal yacht),
the Duke of Norfolk, Earl Grey, Robert Louis Stevenson — the list
of visitors goes on. Iona, even in its desolation, continued to draw
the famous and the curious.

In 1828 Iona became a Church of Scotland parish in its own right,
and it was decided to build a new church designed by the famous
Telford. Thus Iona had a resident pastor again. In 1843 the Iona
parish minister, the Revd Donald Macvean, was among the signatories
to the Act of Separation which established the Free Church of
Scotland. Another church and manse were built adjoining Martyrs
Bay, remaining in service until the reunion of the two branches of
Presbyterianism in 1929.

As the tourists and pilgrims grew in numbers, so did the clamour to
do something about the ruins of the Abbey. George Douglas Campbell,
eighth Duke of Argyll, spent money on the stones and published an
essay on the history and importance of Iona.

In 1899, the Duke gifted the ruins of the Abbey and nunnery, as
well as the Reilig Odhran, to Church of Scotland trustees, with the
far-seeing proviso that the Abbey church should be restored and that
all branches of the Christian Church should be able to worship there.

By 1910 the sanctuary, the place of worship, had been beautifully
restored. The rest of the buildings, the place where the everyday
common life was lived, were still in ruins — symbolizing a cared-for
church in the midst of a world which was heading for the hell of two
world wars. What was needed was a complete rebuilding.

Part Two

FLYING IN FORMATION

4

New Island Soldiers

Another time, another place, another voyage. The year is 1938.

As the boat carries men from Glasgow to Iona for a new experiment in Christian community, the cry of another bird may be heard faintly through the screams of the seagulls. Some of the men find their minds are not on lofty spiritual themes: they are being sick over the side of the boat in choppy seas.

The leader of the group, like Columba in his forty-second year, is making his own peregrination for the love of Christ, his own 'exile', seeking the place of his resurrection. His name is George Fielden MacLeod.

George MacLeod was born on 17 June 1895 into a distinguished family which produced five Moderators of the General Assembly of the Church of Scotland. Son of Sir John MacLeod, Conservative MP, and Lady Edith MacLeod, he was educated at Winchester, Oxford and Edinburgh.

As a young captain in the Argyll and Sutherland Highlanders in the First World War, he distinguished himself by bravery in the field, and was awarded the Military Cross and the Croix de Guerre. The experiences in the Ypres mud made a deep impression on him, however, and he decided to study for ordination. In later years, as he reflected on these war experiences in the light of his Christian faith, he became a pacifist.

In 1926, after completing his theological studies, the young minister joined the staff of St Cuthbert's Church in the centre of Edinburgh. This busy church, with a Sunday school of three thousand youngsters, was a notable preaching centre. George MacLeod, with his aristocratic bearing, commanding presence, charisma and passionate conviction, quickly became known as one of the outstanding young preachers in Scotland. In 1930, he accepted a call to become minister of Govan Old Parish Church, Glasgow. It was a life-changing decision.

Govan Old was sited on holy ground. St Constantine, friend of St Columba and St Mungo, had had his church there fourteen hundred years ago. Govan had been important before Glasgow was heard of, now it was part of that large city. (If the Synod of Whitby had decided in favour of the Celtic Church, the village of Glasgow would today be a suburb of the city of Govan.) Govan was well known as one of the great shipbuilding centres of Britain, but the Depression of the Hungry Thirties had put paid to that. The yards were silent and their skilled craftsmen stood at street corners, wondering how to make ends meet.

George MacLeod set out with characteristic enthusiasm and organizational flair to make the Church relevant to the needs of Govan in the thirties. He organized a mission of friendship. He and his team of volunteers climbed tenement stairs, knocked on all the doors in Govan, and preached at street corners. As a result, more than two hundred adults joined the Church, and over two hundred children joined the Sunday school. Dr MacLeod's preaching attracted people from all over Glasgow, and his reputation was enhanced by his regular radio broadcasts.

The young minister was appalled by the social deprivation in Govan and the Church's lack of response. In theological terms he was conservative, but his experiences in the streets and back courts of Govan reinforced his growing socialist views. Debates with Communist activists attracted over a thousand excited people — the arguments still live on in the folklore of Govan.

MacLeod, distressed by the wastage of human skills which mass unemployment brought, invited craftsmen to repair a broken-down mill at Fingleton, near Glasgow, and exulted in the exercise of talents displayed before his eyes. The mill served as a leisure retreat for hard-pressed Govan families. The Church itself did a great deal of social work, helping those who were up against it.

Govan Old was an example of a very lively parish church under a dynamic and respected minister. But MacLeod knew in his heart of hearts, even at the height of his success, that something more radical needed to be done. Churches were busy, clean, in good order; the communities round about were in ruins. Churches were Sunday affairs, for the good of the soul; what was needed was a faith which penetrated to the heart of the common life. The Church preached an individual salvation which left untouched the deep-rooted problems of the corporate world. No wonder the disillusioned masses voted with their feet! As the war clouds gathered over Europe, MacLeod felt that radical changes were needed if the Church was to speak a word to the modern world. But what to do?

'Come to Iona', a spirit, or a Wild Goose, seemed so say, 'and do it in the round.'

Iona? He had visited the island several times on holiday, and its stirring Christian story appealed to his romantic spirit. To a man who thought in vivid pictures, the Columban imagery was powerful.

His sister, Mrs Ellen Murray, and his senior assistant, Dr Harry Whitley, both suggested that he do a 'Fingleton Mill' and organize the restoration of Iona Abbey. Towards the end of his life George played down his own role, insisting that he was pushed, reluctantly, to implement other people's ideas. He told how he wrote to the Iona Cathedral Trustees, hoping they would refuse to permit any rebuilding:

'To my horror they replied "How marvellous!" They also added in a footnote, "By the way, you will find the money!" I said, "Damn!"'

The truth was a little more complex. As early as 1935, long before any approach to the Cathedral Trustees, the Govan minister had circulated a private paper among a few friends. In it, he said that the Protestant churches were trying to recover their catholic heritage: part of this heritage was the collective witness of the Church, and that witness should not be left solely to the Roman Catholic Church. He also argued that, as large parts of the population of urban Scotland moved out to new housing schemes, the Church of Scotland should develop ministerial teams and teach people how to live corporately. New specialist chaplaincies were also urgently needed if the Church was to make a relevant witness.

At the end of the paper, MacLeod proposed the establishment of a 'brotherhood within the Church of Scotland, of no permanent vows, into which men of such a mind could come for the first two or three years of their ministry'. The first six months after leaving college would be spent in community life: they would then be ready 'to be drafted out — still as members of the brotherhood — to the congested areas and the housing schemes where they would carry their ideas into practice'.

The base for the new brotherhood would be Iona, and unemployed craftsmen would be invited to restore the ancient Abbey buildings. 'It would be the modern counterpart of St Columba's original intention: the New Light of Protestantism would be lit to meet our day, as his Lamp met his.'

In a footnote, MacLeod added, 'I understand that the late Duke of Argyll refused over £100,000 for the island from representatives of the Roman Church. What they would have made of the island had they obtained it, we all know well. As in fact the Church of Scotland holds it, is there not a duty upon us to make more use of it — or at least to attempt to make more use of it — than so far we as a Church have contrived to do?'

In this hitherto unpublished paper, the genesis of the Iona Community can be seen. George MacLeod reflected, discussed, prayed and in 1938 sent to the Iona Cathedral Trustees what is, in effect, the founding document of the Iona Community. It is a systematic elaboration of the earlier paper. In addition to talking about the needs of adequate staffing for housing scheme churches and a training in corporate life (to make up for the deficiencies of the theological colleges), MacLeod argued that the Presbyterian witness of the Church was at stake in Scotland. The whole Reformed scheme of private and corporate worship was in danger of collapse, and a new experiment had to be made.

> Is the truth not that the old cultus has splendidly served its day and generation; it is our modern environment that has rendered it outmoded. It is not the old Reformation timbers that are in criticism, it is that they survive from a day of wooden houses. It is not the building of the old channels that has rendered them faulty, but the shifting of the subsoil of this evolving world.

Declaring that the Church must draw on only the best of its historical tradition, he went on:

How up-to-date was the enthusiasm of the early
Celtic Church to infuse with the Christian spirit every
department of life; how like the most modern foreign
mission station was the early Celtic community with
its expert craftsmen, its expert agriculturalist, its
educationist and doctor, as well as its — more strictly
religious — personal therapist (anamchara) and
presiding minister. How much again, is the world not
in need of that sense of Universal Church which was
so profound a belief in our own Roman days.

What is needed, says the writer, is not a new book, but a new
experiment. Young ministers would act as labourers for craftsmen
restoring Iona Abbey, and in so doing would be trained to work
together in ministry in difficult places. The document closes with the
offer which made the experiment possible:

For the purpose of its inception, I would myself be
prepared to leave my present work at any time now
and I would undertake to stand by the Experiment
full time, resisting any conceivable inducements, for
a term of five years. For such time during that period
as I remained unmarried, I would offer my services
without reward, but would ask for the payment of
my essential expenses when travelling in the name of
the Brotherhood.

In its origins, then, the Iona Community was essentially an
experiment to train Church of Scotland ministers for ministry in the
new urban Scotland. If not exactly anti-Roman Catholic, it was
certainly strongly Presbyterian.

Yet it was more than that. Its association with the inspiration of
Iona and the Celtic tradition — and with all that meant in the latent
memory of Scotland — plus the fact that it was the brainchild of a
conservative, radical, charismatic, impatient, imperious, romantic,
iconoclastic, passionate man of oratory and action who, like Columba,
could inspire others to join him on wild goose projects, meant that
the Iona Community could never be simply categorized.

Men quickly caught the vision and accepted George MacLeod's
challenge, especially in the light of his willingness to give up the
security of his ministry in Govan (amidst much headshaking). Money

had to be found quickly, but from what sources? George recollected in tranquillity:

> I wrote to the richest man I knew. He replied, 'You
> must have gone off your head!' Then I wrote to the
> second richest man I knew, but he hasn't replied yet:
> and as that was fifty years ago I don't suppose he will
> now. Then I wrote to Sir James Lithgow. He had a
> shipbuilding yard right beside my parish church. I
> asked him for £5000. He invited me to spend the
> night. This surprised me because we were not very
> close: he was building battleships and I was already a
> pacifist. Actually I asked him because I thought he
> would refuse, and that would finish my appealing.
> But before I left, he asked, 'If I give you £5000, Will
> you give up your pacifism?' 'Not on your life,' I
> replied. Then he said, 'Then I will give you £5000!'
> So I was properly caught out, and was now
> committed.

Thus it was that in July 1938 the *Dunara Castle* steamed into the Sound of Iona, bearing vomiting divinity students and craftsmen. Three weeks earlier, an advance party had erected wooden huts alongside the ruins.

In the first issue of *The Coracle* [later it would become simply *Coracle*], a magazine published in October to answer the multitude of questions being asked, George MacLeod wrote:

> It was a slightly dazed company — truth to tell —
> who sat down for their first meal together out in the
> open, beneath the old Abbey and beside the solitary
> log cabin that was to be their dormitory, sitting and
> dining room for the next three months! Few knew
> more than two of the others previously, the majority
> were sitting in a community of complete strangers.
> Had we been too hurried? Would we all get on
> together? As we looked at the size of the hut, some
> must have wondered. But as we looked at the Abbey
> we were reminded that the whole purpose of the
> experiment was to prove that what it stood for still
> worked.

So the new community on Iona began its life, worshipping twice daily in the ancient Abbey (using a form of worship adapted from the daily liturgy at Govan Old) and working together on the restoration of the ruined library. The young ordinands learned about working with their hands and about communication with working men. Their leader wrote:

> High Church and Low Church seemed absurdly trivial subjects now to excite much conversation from the parsons. The questions of the artisans were of a more fundamental thrust and some of us — who thought we were old hands — were reminded for the hundredth time what nonsense most of our sermons must sound. The parson who was heard in the first week attempting to clarify an argument with the actual words, 'your premise having fallen, your conclusion is false' (which so clarified the argument that it stopped altogether) was the centre of an argument in autumn that evaded such atrocities and was clarified by simplicity. And time and time again we were reminded that artisans are better men than parsons — not just at their jobs but at piercing through by instinct to those real issues which mental acrobatics so often utterly confuse.

It felt right to be living in community on Iona, in continuity with the Columban and the Benedictine communities. Living in cramped quarters and sharing with others brought home the essentially corporate nature of Christian faith and made the corporate language of the New Testament and the Early Church come alive. Ministers and craftsmen, sharing in a situation in which they depended on one another, found new insights into the nature of the Gospel. The essentially individualistic nature of Christianity presented in the nineteenth and twentieth centuries was seen to be inadequate. The problem facing the Church was similar to that confronting the world: how to live corporately, sharing life and its resources in a spirit of interdependence, while preserving the rights of the individual.

The experiment on the island was regarded with suspicion on the mainland, particularly within the national Church of Scotland. Who were these people? Were they playing at monks? Were they muddled romantics? Were they practising a form of Communism? Were they crypto-Roman Catholics in Presbyterian guise? Were they political radicals and pacifists out to undermine the social order? As rumours grew about the weekly celebration of the sacrament, responses in worship, candles in the Abbey and political discussion, the controversy increased. The Community was accused of being half way towards Rome and half way towards Moscow. The huts outside the Abbey were nicknamed 'The Rome Express'.

George MacLeod defended the new-born project in *The Coracle*. It was *not* a return to Rome. It was *not* a pacifist community. It was *not* a visionary movement, playing at being monks.

> It is, on the contrary, an exceedingly calculated movement within the normal purpose of the Church. Poverty is not our aim, far less is the principle of celibacy involved. Those who come here will claim no 'sacrifice'; we only claim a privilege to make perhaps the sacrifice of those who work in really difficult places a little less acute.

At the end of an exhausting but exhilarating summer, the men returned to the mainland to resume their studies or look for work. The latest Iona Community experiment was well and truly under way.

5

Birds of Prey

In Europe a much more radical experiment was about to begin. Wild geese were not the only birds to be seen in the darkening sky: the vultures of hatred, already feeding greedily on the casualties of unemployment and recession and the fantasies of a kingdom that would last for a thousand years, prepared to swoop for a delicious slaughter. The seagulls over Iona were in for a thin time.

What was to be done? Should the fragile island experiment be shelved until a more propitious time? Many thought so. The press informed the public of the demise of the project, but Captain George MacLeod, MC, stood firm. His clear view was that a time of war

> should call forth from such spiritual ventures as the Iona Community not a battening of the hatches, but rather a crowding on of more canvas. There is not a purpose for which it stands, the need of whose prosecution is not made more insistent by the probabilities before us. Should the war be shortened, all the problems referred to will emerge again with gathered potency; should the war be long, the problems with which almost delicately we were dealing will be found to challenge us as stark imperatives. The problem is not whether the Community should continue, but into what new channels it should regulate its forces.

Dr MacLeod then proposed that a modified building programme should proceed, involving the craftsmen only. Since it was unlikely that any young ministers worth their salt would apply to spend three months on Iona in the midst of a world war, he made a suggestion that would radically alter the life and direction of the young and vulnerable community: twelve weeks of conference and retreat would be offered to clergy, divinity students and laity, using the huts as accommodation. Thus early on, by the pressure of outside events rather than original intention, Iona became a place of study, community learning and training in discipleship for the wider Church.

But what of the more intensive experiment in common living for young ordinands? It was decided to move base to the historic Canongate Kirk in Edinburgh, where the minister, the Revd Dr R. Selby Wright, had offered his house for use by the Community. Dr Wright, who as a senior chaplain to the armed forces went on to become well-known as the wartime 'Radio Padre', wrote for his pacifist friend a collect which, in updated form, is still the official prayer of the Iona Community:

> God our Father, who didst give unto Thy servant, Columba, the gifts of courage, faith and cheerfulness and didst send men forth from Iona to carry the Word of Thine Evangel to every creature; grant, we beseech Thee, a like spirit to Thy Church in Scotland, even at this Present time. Further in all things the purpose of the New Community, that hidden things may be revealed to them and new ways found to touch the hearts of men. May they preserve with each other sincere charity and peace and, if it be Thy holy will, grant that a place of Thine Abiding be established once again to be a Sanctuary and a Light. Through Jesus Christ our Lord. Amen.

An anonymous donor offered to pay for four teams of two ministers to go to the new housing schemes for six years. After its first fifteen months of existence, the Iona Community, which, according to its leader, was formed 'as a handmaid of the organized Church to specialize in meeting the needs of a rapidly changing day', was in a position to offer the national Church of Scotland ministers (by then twelve in number) trained to work in teams in needy places.

Those who joined the Community received the same rate of pay as a serving soldier. In addition to the housing schemes, men were offered for the Church of Scotland army huts and canteens (which served tea to soldiers) and for country charges where evacuees brought new problems.

As a pacifist, George MacLeod was under attack at a time when the nation was at war. He defended his Community, which already had within its membership both men destined for the army and pacifists.

> The Community is neither pacifist nor non-pacifist. Anything we form on the mainland must have its doors open to all — as any Church has anyway. But just as our soldier members would be untrue to themselves if they now resigned from the army, I must also record that I feel I would be untrue to myself if I now renounced the views I hold . . . The one supreme conviction that I cannot get away from and — without any dramatics — am quite willing to die for, is that only the spiritual can mould any future worth having for the world.

It is interesting to note the military precision with which events on the mainland and island were organized. Reveille was at 6.45 a.m., and the day was fully structured until 'cocoa and lights out' at 10.30 p.m. The former cavalry officer spoke to his men in military metaphors. The new Island Soldiers were described as an 'advance party' for the main body of the Church. Men living together in the huts on Iona constantly compared their experiences with the mess and the barracks. Let it not be said that life in the early days of the Iona Community was either easy or frivolous.

However, it was not all serious, either. Cameron Wallace, who became a member in 1939, recalled:

> Our time on Iona was unforgettable. The weather was wonderful, the work was hard, and the ministers and craftsmen worked and lived well together. After hot working days, we went together for a bathe in the Sound just below the Abbey — much to the consternation of female visitors. Like dervishes we rushed in, quite scuddy!

The Community adopted a uniform of dark blue double-breasted suits, blue shirt and blue tie — intended as a reflection of the dress of island fishermen. Cameron Wallace remembered:

> Months before the commissioning service, George MacLeod asked for measurements for the famous blue serge suits, to be made up by the Co-op. Measurements got out of hand, and on fitting out just prior to the service, the scene was laughable — long sleeves, short sleeves, long trouser legs, short trouser legs. Being adaptable fellows, we switched round and exchanged the appropriate garments — by the grace of God or not we were eventually kitted out satisfactorily and made our solemn entry to the Church, suitably dressed, to be known for many a long day as 'Geordie's Fascists'!

Not all the locals appreciated the new blue Island Soldiers. George MacLeod was not noted for his diplomacy, and some saw the project as disturbing the peace of the island. The new Community men went out to visit every island home, and even though many friendships were made, the experiment was viewed at the time with suspicion and even hostility in some quarters.

The venture brought criticism from other places too. George MacLeod remembers:

> A man wrote a letter to *The Scotsman* asking who were these ridiculous men spoiling the peace and beauty of the ruined Abbey with a rotten hut. 'Furthermore,' he wrote, 'they hang out their washing on a Sunday!' I was furious, but did nothing.

> Then I got a letter from a completely unknown lady, supporting me. 'Cleanliness comes next to godliness', she wrote. When I turned the page of her letter, she added that she had always hoped that Iona Abbey would be rebuilt. She enclosed a cheque for £10,000. We always hung out our washing on a Sunday after that!

The restoration continued, but slowly. The library and the chapter house were completed and the reredorter was next. But there was a problem: all timber was now requisitioned for war purposes. George MacLeod again:

> A ship coming over from Canada struck a storm. Her deck cargo was timber: this she jettisoned in the sea for safety, opposite the mouth of the Clyde. This timber floated eighty miles and landed on the coast of Mull exactly opposite Iona — all the right length!

The scenes — with Community men and islanders hauling timber ashore — were reminiscent of *Whisky Galore*. The government allowed the wood to be used on the Abbey, perhaps feeling, nervously, that taking on George MacLeod (and God) was a risky undertaking.

There were critics within the Church who said that rebuilding a medieval ruin was a backward-looking task. In sermons broadcast from the island, the Iona leader replied that the rebuilding had been embarked on partly for its own sake, but more as a symbol of the Church building itself up again with modern material on an old foundation.

'What is the real sickness of this modern world?' he thundered from Iona Abbey pulpit.

> Is it the absence of the Church? I assure you, no! The church was never more efficient than in the days in which we live. Services galore, churches clean and tidy.
>
> But the thing most happens on a Sunday. It is the week-day life of men that lies in ruins. The economic structure — the industrial, the international — these are the grave concerns bereft today of Spirit. These are the places where men have to live and move and have their being — and the roof of them is falling in!

As roofs began to sprout over the common life of Iona Abbey, the number of pilgrims increased. Three thousand people signed up as Friends of the Iona Community, supporting the experiment financially. People came in numbers for the summer courses, to reflect in the context of shared community on what it means to be a Christian in the world. They were delighted to be part of a fellowship which saw prayer and political action as equally important facets of

Christian discipleship and to share in vigorous contemporary worship
in such an inspiring setting.

There were those who wanted a deeper involvement with the Iona
Community. They identified with its purposes and wanted to belong
to a like-minded and supportive fellowship. A branch of Minister
Associates was established, meeting regularly for prayer and
discussion on Iona Community themes. Youth Associates followed,
and then Women Associates.

These developments arose not because the Community planned
them but because hungry people were looking for bread. Some people
in the Church were scandalized by the establishment of Minister
Associates — did the Church at large not offer sufficient fellowship
and support? The answer, sadly, was no. It was a battle to establish
the view that political action for justice and peace was an imperative
of the faith, that the sacraments should be celebrated frequently,
and that responses should be used in a worship which reflected the
priesthood of all believers. People tired of being labelled Communist
or betrayers of the Reformation needed the support of their fellows.
In providing this supportive fellowship, the Iona Community laid
itself open to the charge of setting up a church within the Church.
People who find new insights can often sound — and indeed be self-
righteous and seen as a threatening force. George MacLeod's
combative personality won him and his movement powerful enemies
as well as friends, and ministers who were 'Iona men' could find
themselves blacklisted when they came to apply for charges.

From the perspective of today, the young Community seems
conservative, ecclesiastically speaking. The visible Church is assumed
without question to be the divinely appointed Body of Christ. If the
Church is reformed and renewed, the alienated masses will come in.
The Community repeatedly appeals to history. All the Church has
to do is get it right, and its message and life will prove attractive to
the working classes. However the Iona Community of the 1940s
was not felt by the Church at large to be a conservative body. Though
the General Assembly of the Church of Scotland officially
commended the experiment, the Community was often viewed as a
heretical threat and an irritant.

It must not be imagined that the Community itself was always at
the cutting edge of radical thought. Its military style and all-male
ethos were challenged by women who came to Iona and were

attracted by the ideals of the Community. They kept knocking on the door and refused to be put off. The literature of the time gives the impression that the eventual establishment of Women Associates was a reluctant concession rather than a heart-felt desire for justice and equality. Nor must it be imagined that the peace-loving Community was always peaceable. One of the Community's endearing and sometimes maddening traits has always been its love of argument, especially over the finer points of radical politics. Spades were called by their proper names as pacifist argued with non-pacifist. Columba's holy isle resounded with the echoes of raised voices as the latest scheme for the immediate salvation of the world was unfolded. All, however, preferred it to the polite silence of ecclesiastical inoffensiveness.

George MacLeod's autocratic and impatient style was not appreciated by all. The first person to leave the Community told the leader that it was due to his spelling deficiencies.

'What do you mean?' asked George.

'You should spell it "I own a community"', retorted the brave rebel.

As new members went out to work in the mission field of urban Scotland, the Community was compelled to ask what it was that bound members to each other. Out of these discussions emerged the beginnings of a Rule of Life for the Iona Community. The first obligation was that members had at least half an hour of private prayer each day, using the Church of England revised lectionary and a common prayer-sheet. Private and personal prayer had been an important part of the life of the Iona Community since its inception.

The second part of the rule committed members to planning their day before 8 a.m. This obligation grew out of discussions on the abbey walls between ministers and craftsmen. The masons taunted the ministers with working only on Sundays.

'Oh no,' retorted God's anointed, 'we work eighteen hours a day.'

'When you go back to your parishes,' said the craftsmen, 'take a note of how long you actually work, and don't include things like reading the newspaper, and lying in bed pretending you are meditating.'

The ministers had to concede that, unlike the workmen, they didn't have to clock in and out and were accountable to no boss; this could easily lead to self-delusion and indulgence. On the other hand, a conscientious minister, faced with a never-ending demand, could work himself into an early grave. What was needed was accountability in the proper use of time.

The final thrust of the Iona Community rule dealt with the use of money. Every member was asked to experiment by seeking to live on the National Average — the average annual income as determined by the government. Each member was given a sheet entitled Miles Christi (Soldier of Christ), to record daily how time and money had been spent.

The Community really struggled with economics, particularly after Lex Miller, who had lived in a community in New Zealand, became deputy leader. They knew it was easy, and cheap, to stand up in a pulpit and preach about the responsible use of money. But this was precisely the problem: the Church was good at making spiritual statements in a holy sanctuary and not so good at specifics. The notion that Christians should actually be accountable to each other in how they spent their money was foreign, and indeed offensive, to the Church. The Community argued that in a world in which capitalism seemed to be accountable to no one and caused untold damage, the Church was called upon to provide a pattern of sharing under the sign of the lordship of Christ. Members of the Community agreed to give five per cent of their income to the Church, and five per cent to the Community, of which half went to poorer members of the brotherhood.

Mutual accountability could easily lead to self-righteousness, as people debated whether it was right to spend money on butter, but the Community knew in its heart that the use of money and time was an indication of real, rather than stated, priorities. And prayer was a necessity, not a luxury, if this kind of disciplined life were to be led.

George MacLeod stated provocatively that God had raised up Karl Marx because the Church had failed to address the money question. 'It was for the Crown Rights of the Redeemer that the Covenanters fell,' he declared,

> 'not just for the Comforting Rights of the Redeemer.
> It was for Christ at the centre as King of Kings and
> Lord of Lords: and not just at the periphery as Master
> of Marriages and President of Funerals.'

The Community continued to produce young men to work in teams in urban situations. They worked hard and helped nurture thriving congregations in the new housing areas. A 'Community' parish would have a mission of friendship, responsive worship, more frequent sacraments and an involvement of local Christians in the social and political life of the community round about. Whatever critics in the Church might say, no one could argue with the Community's track record in providing ministers for churches at the sharp end of the social and political divide in Scotland.

On Iona, the buildings continued to take shape. In the early days, a man in hiking gear had appeared on Iona to look at the buildings. He turned out to be Bill Amos, a master mason, and he stayed for many years. Calum MacPherson of Mull became master of works and, with Ian Lindsay, the architect, ensured that the restoration was of high quality. The unheralded heroes of the rebuilding were the craftsmen who worked through the winter, out of the summer spotlight.

By the end of the war, the library, chapter house and reredorter had been restored. The refectory block simply awaited a roof, as did the kitchen. Work on the West Range dormitory was assured by an anonymous gift of £10,000 and a gift of £3,500 had been received for the restoration of the abbot's house.

'We do not seek Christ in the ruins,' said George MacLeod, 'we find Him in the fellowship.'

> Together on wall and in Abbey we seek to forge a new vocabulary of work and worship.

> The nature of a new order will be revealed not by the searchlight of high-powered brains, but in response to the obedience of convinced believers. For Christ is a Person to be trusted, not a principle to be tested. The Church is a movement, not a meeting house. The faith is an experience, not an exposition. Christians are explorers, not map makers. And the new social order is not a blueprint which someone must find quickly. It is a present experience made possible at Bethlehem, offered on Calvary and communicated at Pentecost.

As peace came to an exhausted Europe, it was clear to the churches that only a practical form of Christianity would do. Men and women who had engaged in a hard and co-operative war effort would not be much impressed by rhetoric or a private piety which did nothing about injustice.

Among the signs of hope amid the ruins stood the half-built walls of an abbey on a small island. Pointing out that Iona was a place that all Christians could call home, George MacLeod, moved by the impact of the experiment on the ordinary, seeking people who had come for summer programmes, looked forward:

> It is our hope that the Abbey will be completed as a laboratory school of Christian living where large numbers will come to pray and to confer. It is our instinct that the essentials for which we seek, with many others, to stand will soon become the subjects round which the whole Church will be forced to confer. It is our prayer that, increasingly, in such conferring we will have gatherings in Iona drawn from many denominations and will together glimpse the day when, as in St Columba's time, Christ's Church will be One in every land.

People were beginning to see a potential in the Iona experiment which had not been glimpsed at the beginning.

6

Glory to God in the High Street

The ship from Norway that appeared on the horizon was not bringing men of war. Its cargo was timber, beautiful Scandinavian timber, for the refectory of Iona Abbey. It was the gift of Church and industry in Norway, as reparation for the Viking raids on the island a thousand years earlier!

Signs of international interest in the Iona experiment were matched by the growing number of pilgrims in the post-war era. Reconstruction was in the air, and new movements were springing up within the European churches. There was a growing desire to wed the spiritual to the material, together with a recognition that changes could only be accomplished by mutually supportive groups.

The war had transformed the young Iona movement. What had begun as a self-contained scheme for the training of Presbyterian clergy had developed into an educational programme for people of many denominations. This unforeseen development was matched by another unplanned step which radically altered the life of the Iona Community itself. It had never been intended that the Iona Community would be a permanent group with continuity of membership. Its purpose was simply to train young men for team ministry — and after their two years' service they would seek a church post of their own and leave the Community. However, when the men moved out on their own, they found they missed the fellowship and support of like-minded comrades. So why not remain as full members of the Iona Community, bound together by the common rule of life? This was agreed. The consequence was that instead of remaining a small community of men in training, it grew in numbers and inexperience. Men from other denominations and other countries also sought to join in this very hopeful venture. Thus, somewhat bewilderingly, the Iona Community found itself responsible for a much larger and wider network of people than it could ever have bargained for. By 1947 there were five thousand seven hundred signed-up Friends.

What was the attraction! Obviously Iona, with its inspiring history. Clearly the vision of the confident and committed MacLeod. Certainly the relief of finding a group which refused to hive off prayer and politics into separate compartments. But above all, an experiment which put its body where its soul was. As usual, Dr MacLeod put the matter vividly and memorably:

> Not all the honeyed words of the greatest preachers will by themselves recall men to the true recovery. Nor would the perfect pamphlet, written by the Archangel Gabriel himself and laid at every churchman's door, resolve the dichotomy or correct the divorce. Only by the portrayal of the Word, alongside its preaching, will men regain once more the true proportions. The Iona Community is but one cradle for the rebirth of a consciousness of that total Salvation which is the original Gospel Word. The Iona Community is no more than a 'John the Baptist' movement in preparation for a new coming of the Lord.

That sense of expectancy communicated itself particularly to young people. They made their way to Iona — not the easiest of places to get to — because they sensed that something important was happening. Again, this development was not in the script. The notion that the Community masterminded all these changes is laughable: time and again they were taken by surprise and had no plan to deal with the situation.

One answer was to rent a salmon-fishing station at Camas on Mull, on a bay opposite Iona, and run youth camps there. A group of boys from Rugby School got the buildings in order. A chapel was made, furnished with barrels and fishing nets. University students and schoolboys came to Camas and sailed to Iona for Communion and a meal each Sunday. During the week they worked on building and fishing — George MacLeod registered as a retail fishmonger in order to sell the Camas salmon!

The biblical imagery of fishing featured in many a Camas meditation: the fact that the salmon was a Celtic symbol for wisdom did not go unnoticed either. Camas became used more and more as a centre for delinquent youngsters from Borstals. They were allowed to come to Camas for a week, experiencing fishing, outdoor activities, discussion and, if they wished, worship. For many of the youngsters it proved to be a life-changing experience. The low-key Camas work with delinquent youngsters, though not popular locally at first, was one of the most important enterprises organized by the Iona Community, although it has always been overshadowed by the work on Iona itself.

The interest of young people in the Iona Community altered the Community's life and work in totally unforeseen ways. An astonishing gift of £20,000 a year for seven years was made to the Youth Committee of the Church of Scotland, with the express purpose of establishing experiments in youth work along the lines of the Iona Community. The gift, anonymous at the time, was from Sir James and Lady Lithgow. The Iona Youth Trust, which was set up to administer the funds, consisted of representatives of the Church of Scotland Youth Committee, the Iona Community and the donors. It was decided to use the money (a very considerable sum in the mid-1940s) to finance youth camps on Iona, set up three youth centres in congested areas, establish a residence for men coming home from the war who were contemplating training for Christian work, and set up a youth house in Glasgow.

The house at 214 Clyde Street was to be the Glasgow home of the Iona Community for thirty years. Situated on the banks of the River Clyde, near the Glasgow bus station and accessible from all parts of the city, Community House became one of the West of Scotland's best-known meeting places. The Revd Ralph and Jenny Morton became joint wardens of the house. They had served for ten years in the Presbyterian mission in China before Ralph became minister of St Columba's Church, Cambridge. The couple's commitment and talents ensured that Community House got off to the best possible start.

In the immediate postwar years, hope and determination to build a new and more just world were in the air. The Labour government's new health, welfare and housing programmes had the broad consent of the country. The corporate war effort had changed notions of what was or was not possible. The discussion of radical ideas and the quest for knowledge meant that places like Community House had no difficulty in attracting people. The house, with its restaurant, open chapel, library and meeting space, was an ideal base.

It was the unusual mixture of religious inspiration and radical politics which made Community House such an interesting and vital place. Classes in faith, politics, industrial affairs, films and drama were well subscribed. Oliver Wilkinson, who was appointed to take charge of drama, staged several plays in Glasgow. The first was based on George MacLeod's book, *We Shall Rebuild*, which explained the ideas behind the Iona Community and sold twenty thousand copies when published by the Community's new publishing department. Drama was used as a vehicle for religious and political ideas through street theatre and shows in local halls.

Alice Scrimgeour, youth clubs organizer, and David Orr, senior youth adviser, brought young people to the house for training. Their methods followed those of the Christian Workers League which had been established by the Iona Community in 1943. Biblical study and social and political analysis were followed by action in local situations. As the controversial political and industrial work continued, the demand for education grew, and Penry Jones was appointed full-time industrial secretary. Trades unions and management came together to discuss matters of mutual concern and conflict. Theological students, after a spell in Iona, went to work in industry and reflect on their experiences. It was out of this creative ferment that the Church of Scotland Home Board's industrial work grew.

Community House in the 1940s and 50s affected the lives of many people in the West of Scotland. It was a place of hospitality and welcome as well as of education and controversy. The Scottish folk music movement found a home: Robin Hall, Jimmie MacGregor and friends were often to be found there, as were budding politicians such as Jimmy Reid, Bruce Millan, George Thomson and Dickson Mabon. What impressed many people was the openness and vigour of the place — the unembarrassed talk of religion and politics contrasting with the bland inoffensiveness of much conventional church life. Scottish War on Want was founded in Community House, as was the Glasgow Marriage Guidance Council. The caring work was extended by the founding of Gamblers' Anonymous in

Community House, which also became a refuge for alcoholics, down and outs and victims of violence.

Community House complemented what was being done in parishes by Iona Community ministers who, after their summer training on Iona, went out to serve what George MacLeod termed 'apprenticeships in difficult places'. Inner city areas and housing schemes benefited as the Community continued to attract very able young men from the divinity colleges. These were still the days of stability in church membership, with the Church of Scotland claiming over one million members out of a population of five million. Families who were moved out from inner-city slums to the green, green grass of the new housing schemes on the perimeter of the cities were often prepared to make the Church a part of their new start. The ministers who went to these charges were by no means all Iona Community men, but the Community made a substantial contribution.

The decision of the Iona Youth Trust to finance youth camps on Iona was far-reaching for the life and witness of the Community. Many young people went, particularly from inner-city and housing-scheme parishes, and lived in tents at the north end of the island or in a camp at the village. They shared in the twice-daily worship of the Abbey, scrubbed their porridge pots in the sea, enjoyed the beauty of the island, debated, socialized and generally had a good time. Impressed by the rebuilding and the reasons for it, young people were challenged by the Christian message as it was preached from the Iona Abbey pulpit or lived out on the Abbey walls. The need for visible commitment to Christ expressed by young people was met by the institution of the 'Act of Belief' Thursday evening service, at which worshippers were given the opportunity to kneel before the marble communion table and commit themselves to Christ, as so many had done in preceding centuries. Many young people came back again and again, and many were able to date important vocational (and matrimonial) decisions from their time on Iona.

Adults came in numbers too. The summer courses on faith, prayer, politics, healing, the Celtic Church, and industry proved popular. Leaders such as R. D. Laing, Donald Mackinnon, John Macmurray, F. W. Dillistone, Charles Raven and John Wren Lewis were stimulating and challenging speakers. But Iona weeks were not simply conferences. Guests were expected to do chores and help with physical work, as well as study, debate and worship. The week was intended to be an experience of shared Christian community, in historic continuity with the Columban and Benedictine communities. This was — and is — the secret of Iona.

Another unforeseen development lay in the area of healing. Iona, as we have seen, had always attracted people seeking healing. Out of the need to respond, there developed a weekly service of prayers for the sick and the laying-on of hands. The Community's theology of healing was not one of magic intervention, but of the corporate care of the Church in obedience to Jesus. Healing, like prayer, could not be separated from politics — it was not enough to pray for a child dying of tuberculosis in a damp tenement slum.

The pattern of a typical Iona experience of community gradually took shape. Worship, work, study, discussion, socializing, healing, commitment, communion were all of a piece. At the heart of each week was the Wednesday pilgrimage round the island stopping for worship and reflection at the marble quarry, Columba's Bay, the machair (common grazing ground), the Hermit's Cell, Dun I (the highest point on the island), and the Reilig Odhrain. The pilgrimage combined appreciation of the wonder of creation, stories, history and faith.

Above all, the message of the Iona experience was that the faith had to be lived in the world. Iona itself was a laboratory, an experiment, a retreat, a place of inspiration and a mission training station; but the Christian's place was as a member of community living in a wider community.

The Iona Community did not see itself as having a theology of its own, it was not an alternative church. Its creeds were those of the national Church of Scotland; it did, however, have particular emphases.

The doctrine most emphasized by the Community was that of the Incarnation — the coming of God to humanity in the shape of Jesus Christ. God, in love, had entered the human situation in all its mess and glory. Humanity had thus been dignified and ennobled. The spiritual had been joined to the material in Jesus Christ, and the material could therefore never be despised. Since the face of Jesus was to be discerned in the poor, the hungry, the prisoners and the victims, social and political action could never be divorced from spirituality.

'The Gospel claims the key to all material issues', wrote George MacLeod, 'is to be found in the mystery that Christ came in a body:

and healed bodies and fed bodies: and that He died bodily and Himself rose in His body, to save Man body and soul.'

In his book, *Only One Way Left*, consisting of the Cunningham Lectures delivered in Edinburgh and New York, Dr MacLeod used an illustration which neatly summed up his view of the Incarnation and its implications:

> A boy threw a stone at the stained glass window of the Incarnation. It nicked out the 'E' in the word HIGHEST in the text, 'GLORY TO GOD IN THE HIGHEST'. Thus, till unfortunately it was mended, it read, 'GLORY TO GOD IN THE HIGH ST'.
>
> At least the mended E might have been contrived on a swivel so that in a high wind it would have been impossible to see which way it read. Such is the genius, and the offence, of the Christian revelation. Holiness, salvation, glory are all come down to earth in Jesus Christ our Lord. Truth is found in the constant interaction of the claim that the apex of the Divine Majesty is declared in Christ's humanity. The Word of God cannot be dissociated from the Action of God. As the blood courses through the body, so the spiritual is alone kept healthy in its interaction in the High Street.

In a stunning and oft-quoted paragraph, the Community's founder talked about the relationship of the action of God to High Streets everywhere:

> I simply argue that the Cross be raised again at the centre of the market place as well as on the steeple of the church. I am recovering the claim that Jesus was not crucified in a cathedral between two candles, but on a cross between two thieves; on the town garbage heap; at a crossroad so cosmopolitan that they had to write His title in Hebrew and in Latin and in Greek (or shall we say in English, in Bantu and in Afrikaans!); at the kind of place where cynics talk smut, and thieves curse, and soldiers gamble. Because that is where He died. And that is what He died

about. And that is where churchmen should be and
what churchmanship should be about.

Along with the Incarnation, the Community emphasized the work
of the Holy Spirit. Orthodox though he was, George MacLeod was
an imaginative poet whose Celtic imagery and language pushed the
parameters of orthodoxy. As early as 1942, the memorable themes of
his sermons and prayers in Iona Abbey were prefiguring the themes of
Process Theology and Liberation Theology, which were not to come
to the fore for another twenty or thirty years. There was no such
thing as dead matter, he declared; the whole universe vibrated in
terms that human beings can only glimpse. Since God came in Christ,
there was nothing common or unclean.

> Christ is the light of the World and the life of the
> World. He is the light-energy for our individual needs
> because He is the key to the ultimate nature of all
> existence. And it is He that has made us 'modern men'
> [and women] and brought us into this wilderness,
> that we may drink new streams of 'the rock that is
> Christ', and learn again the meaning of His cosmic
> presence.

> He is the only interpreter but the quite sufficient
> interpreter of our modern impasse. He must somehow
> be declared again to the physical consciousness, the
> scientific inquiry and the social passions of modern
> man [and woman].

> It was God who made modern man [and woman] a
> materialistic creature: and that far from stultifying
> our witness, materialism opens a new and effectual
> door if only we preach the full old Gospel.

MacLeod's theology was worked out and expressed in the context
of worship, which was all-important for the Iona Community. This
was not a theology put together in a study. To be in a seat at Iona
Abbey, to be moved by the awesome oratory of a MacLeod sermon
in full flood, was to be led into the nearer presence of God by means
of kaleidoscopic imagery. It was also to be changed.

Yes, it was orthodox, but it was never static. The Incarnation
implied that ideas were not enough — they had to be embodied,

enfleshed. This is what made the Iona Community experiment exciting and drew people to the island in increasing numbers; there were plenty of books and pamphlets about church reform, but precious few living experiments. The experiments in turn helped shape the doctrine. Dr MacLeod commented, 'I believe that in little communities trying, failing and trying again, on their own lines, in their own way, and scorning well-tried paths, there is a secret waiting for us that we, as stale churchmen, can't begin to glimmer.'

Arguing that movement should be the permanent mark of any organization that claimed to be the Church, the Iona leader went on:

> What the static nature of our faith has clouded out from our perceiving is that Jesus is the only Orthodoxy and never does He stay still.
>
> Doctrine has always emerged out of experience . . . men will listen now only to those who prophetically dare to taste first for them the new revivement: and who dare to be the shape of things to come.
>
> To determine on the practice of community is to go into a mist, and to be lost, and to wish one had stayed closer to the maps before going out: but it is the only Orthodoxy left for this age of the world. It is the grand and final test for any man [or woman] as to whether 'Jesus is'.

The mixture of radical politics, a Catholic sense of the Church and the sacraments, a cosmic view of Christ as the light-energy of the world, and the notion of Christ as the heart of a continually moving orthodoxy — all part of a community restoring a medieval Abbey while claiming pure Presbyterian pedigree — was too much for some people. MacLeod and the Iona Community were accused of being heretical.

The hostility came out repeatedly on the floor of the General Assembly of the Church of Scotland. Strict consitutionalists argued that there was no place for such a strange community within Presbyterianism; it was a private group which could have no relationship with the Kirk. The matter came to a head when his old congregation at Govan asked George MacLeod to go back as their minister. He was willing to do so, prepared now to give up active leadership of the well-founded Iona experiment. The discussion in Glasgow Presbytery was sometimes bitter. Their decision: Dr MacLeod could not accept the call as he was the leader of a community which was outside the jurisdiction of the Church of Scotland. In 1949 the case went to the General Assembly, which supported the Presbytery's ruling.

As a strong churchman, George MacLeod found the decision hurtful, yet it was an almost inevitable consequence of the way in which the Iona Community was founded in 1938. If he had been patient, diplomatic and tactful, he might have persuaded the Kirk to take the idea on board and give official permission for the setting up of the new experiment — but the process could have taken years. Since he was neither patient, diplomatic nor tactful — and had he been, Iona Abbey would probably still be in ruins today — the clash with Presbyterian polity had to come.

There were many people in the Assembly who, while not supporters of the Community, recognized its worth and wished it to come within the jurisdiction of the Kirk. In 1951 the situation was resolved with the setting up of the Iona Community Board. The Community reported to the General Assembly each year, yet retained control over its own policy making and finances.

So, thirteen years after its foundation, the Iona experiment was accepted — or tolerated — as part of the Church. The *enfant terrible* was growing up — but into what?

7

Travelling On and Reaching Out

Radical movements face a special danger when they are applauded, admired, copied and, ever so gently, co-opted. In the 1950s the Iona Community entered such dangerous territory.

As knowledge of the work of the Community increased and as its influence grew, pilgrims came to Iona in ever-increasing numbers. A new centre at Kirkridge in the USA had already been established on the Iona model, and the Community inspired a number of similar projects. Representatives from churches in Europe and America came to see what was going on. Although there was still considerable hostility, the Community began to be seen much more as part of the mainstream of the Church's witness rather than part of the lunatic and heretical fringe. The first report of the Iona Community Board to the General Assembly of the Church of Scotland described the Community as an agency of the Church of Scotland which existed

> to find ways and means to bring to fruition in our congregations those many injunctions and recommendations that are now the commonplaces of the higher courts of our Church and those constant advices that come to us alike from the British and the World Council of Churches . . .

The Iona Community claims justification for its

> existence as a separate agency of the Church not on
> the grounds that it says new things, but because there
> is required a separate organism to discover how these
> things are to be said.

The language is, of course, political, designed to disarm criticism; but the ice is a little thin.

The Community could in no way be perceived as a voice crying in the wilderness. The development of the Evangelical Academies and the Kirchentag (a huge church gathering) in Germany, the Worker Priest movement in France, Ted Wickham's industrial mission in Sheffield, and the 'Tell Scotland' movement were but a few signs of a resurgent concern for mission and education within the churches. The Iona Community's advocacy of relevant, responsive worship, more frequent celebration of Holy Communion, mission by the whole congregation and industrial mission seemed much less strange in the 1950s. And as Community-trained ministers became involved in the day-to-day concerns of busy parishes, the voices advocating reform became less strident, but no less persuasive because of that. The Kirk took up the Community's call for industrial mission, eventually appointing the Revd George Wilkie, an Iona man, as its first industrial organizer.

The restoration work on Iona continued, with the opening of the Refectory in 1953: men sat down to eat there for the first time in over four hundred years. The dormitory block was roofed and furnished, Columba's shrine was restored and the cloisters embarked upon.

Strange things continued to happen. Dr MacLeod saw a big silver-plated Celtic cross in the window of a London shop — just the thing for the Abbey communion table. The woman at the counter told him that it was not for sale: her late husband had heard that Iona Abbey was being rebuilt, and felt that the cross would be just the thing . . .

In 1955, the community moved out of the huts and into the monastic buildings — all under the one roof for the first time. It was also the year of the death of Charlie Kirkpatrick, an islander who had worked for several years as part of the craftsmen's team. He was killed unloading timber from a puffer at Martyrs Bay.

In 1956 the Queen visited the Abbey, together with the Duke of Edinburgh and Princess Margaret. ('Who are these sinister men dressed in dark clothes?' asked the young princess, as she eyed the Community members in the choir stalls.) The Queen had given an oak screen to the Abbey on the occasion of her marriage, at a time when the Community was under severe criticism. Special ferries had brought more than a thousand people to the island and as many as possible crammed into the ancient Abbey for Sunday morning worship.

The Queen listened intently as Dr MacLeod said in his sermon that the religion of Columba and of Benedict was corporate, concerned with all life, with whole salvation rather than with soul salvation. Their religion was concerned as much with agriculture as with anxieties; as much with high politics and their right direction as with the pieties.

> I only know that if we are to make it, then we must call back Columba, who insisted the Faith had to do with history and not just with hysteria. We must call back the Benedictines, who insisted on one Church (and we must not be content with our miserable divisions as our witness — God forgive us — to reconciliation! Why should men listen to our advice on reconciliation till we ourselves unite?) Yes, and we must call back the Reformers, with their insistence on personal commitment.

The Iona Community leader was invited by churches in several countries to lecture and tell the story of the new Community. He travelled to Australia and New Zealand, and spent a year as visiting professor at Union Theological Seminary in New York (where he had spent a postgraduate year in 1924). His verbal jousts with the great Reinhold Niebuhr are still fondly remembered, and it is recorded that he gave a hundred and thirty-four talks about the Iona Community. In 1956 the Community published his American lectures as *Only One Way Left* — a passionate call for justice as the expression of Christian faith. He dedicated the book to his charming wife Lorna, whom he had married in 1948, in the words, 'Dedicated to my wife, who is always Right'.

In 1957 George MacLeod became Moderator of the General Assembly of the Church of Scotland — the first nomination to be objected to on the floor of the Assembly. MacLeod and controversy seemed to go together, but his enormous gifts could not be denied by the Church.

Amidst all this busyness and attention, the Iona Community was growing. Ministers from different denominations and countries became full members, spending three months labouring for the craftsmen before going out to parishes. People came from many nations to take part in the courses in the Abbey and bring their questions.

One of the insistent questions they brought was, 'Why can't we join the Iona Community?' Ministers could join, of course, but the only laymen were the craftsmen working on the Abbey walls. The number of craftsmen was limited and stable, the number of clerics disproportionately high. This was something which had not been foreseen in the decision to allow ministers to remain full members after their initial training period.

The Community had moved from being a fellowship of ministers-in-training with an equal number of craftsmen, to being a small group of craftsmen with a larger number of ministers. The purpose of this Community was the training of clergy for difficult situations on the mainland. There were tensions — some of the craftsmen felt that, despite the language of participation, they were no more than audio-visual aids for the training of ministers — but the purpose of the enterprise was undeniably clear. If people other than ministers or craftsmen were able to join, what would be the *raison d'être* of the Community?

The development came not because the Community sought it, but because laymen kept knocking on the door. They wanted to be fully part of this exciting experiment: was there any good reason why they should not be? The Community proceeded pragmatically, but in a rather confused manner. Laymen joined and they were quaintly described as craftsmen, as if nothing had really changed. But it had.

The old craftsmen knew their job and their role within the Iona Community. Ministers were members because of their ministry, and the Community spent a great deal of its time discussing what it meant to be a minister in the modern world. There was a cohesion, even if the relationships were somewhat uneasy at times. But a civil engineer such as Albert McAdam, or an industrial manager like Jim Hughes, had other concerns to those of the Iona craftsmen or the ministers.

The new lay members brought richness, diversity, confusion and questions. Should the Community concentrate on the ordained ministry in its strategy for changing the Church? Did it have an informed word for people on the difficult frontiers of industrial life? Was it not, despite its talk, too ecclesiastical? The old cohesion was stretched beyond breaking point. It was no longer quite so simple to say what the Iona Community was all about, or what membership meant. One could no longer point to Iona or the housing schemes and inner-city areas and say, 'There is the Iona Community'. And if members could be scattered geographically and in different jobs, what was it that actually bound them together?

The new questions brought a sympathetic response from Ralph Morton, who was by now deputy leader. Ralph was a good foil for George MacLeod — a canny theologian, gentle, unabrasive. He was no orator, yet his words penetrated, quietly. He was the Salmon to MacLeod's Wild Goose, and the Community benefited from the formidable array of skills offered by the two men.

Ralph Morton had thought deeply about the position of the laity in the Church. Influenced by the burgeoning European laity movements, he felt that churches generally put too much emphasis on the ordained ministry; the problem was how to mobilize and train the whole people of God for mission, and how to train ordained men for this kind of enabling ministry. His books, *The Twelve Together* and *The Household of Faith*, published by the Iona Community, took up these issues and were widely read — as were his later publications in collaboration with Mark Gibbs, *God's Frozen People* and *God's Lively People*. He was concerned to develop a coherent theology of the laity and produce educational methods appropriate to the task in hand.

Dr Morton's thinking was in line with developments within the Iona Community and with the growth in numbers of ordinary church members coming to Iona for the summer programme. He instituted a special commission on the place of the laity in the Iona Community. It recommended that laymen seeking to join the Community as full members should spend a year as Associates, have a minimum of two weeks in residence on Iona in the summer, and for the first two years of membership undertake some special activity in terms of their job or local political or social work.

The new arrangements were entirely appropriate to the new situation — few laymen were in a position to spend three months in the summer on Iona. It did mean, however, that there were now effectively three classes of members: ministers, who spent three months on Iona and worked in teams for two years; craftsmen, who worked all summer on the monastic buildings; and laymen. The Community meant different things to these three groups. Not only that, the ministers who had joined in the beginning were now in parishes of their own, even second parishes, sometimes in the suburbs or rural areas. Minister members from different denominations and different countries brought their own perspectives and concerns. Ministry in the inner-city areas and new housing schemes was no longer the sole focus of the Iona Community, even though by the end of the 1950s a third of the membership of the Community was engaged in ministry in church extension areas.

With divergent concerns and sympathies, what was it that held the expanding community together? The answer is that more attention was paid to the Rule of the Community — the agreement on prayer, planning of time and economic sharing to which each member committed himself every year. But was a community of eighty full members not now too big and diverse for the exercise of mutual accountability? The solution was to divide into regional family groups, in which members and their wives could share in fellowship, discuss matters of mutual concern and report on observance of the Community's Rule.

The Economic Discipline was the most controversial part of the Rule. The Community was not a monastic group of celibates with a standard income. It was increasingly a diverse fellowship of people doing different jobs, earning widely differing salaries and living in different parts of the country. How was it possible to reach an economic agreement which would be fair? The answer came from an experiment devised by the staff of Community House. It was agreed that the annual income tax return should provide the basis: after tax, allowances, rent and rates were deducted, each member should give five per cent of the disposable income which remained to a common fund, distributed by decision of Community members. It was not the perfect solution, but members were compelled to overcome their embarrassment about personal finance and think very hard about their life priorities.

With George MacLeod spending so much time abroad in lecturing, fundraising and Moderatorial duties, Ralph Morton was quite often in charge of the Community. After his Moderatorial year, MacLeod was appointed convener of the Church of Scotland's Church Extension Committee — a very demanding task which he exercised with characteristic enthusiasm and skill. Some members of the Community resented George's appointment, feeling he had been sucked into the maw of the church he had sought to reform.

The issues of *The Coracle* in the late 1950s and early 60s show a marked shift in emphasis. The focus is much less on the rebuilding on Iona and training men for urban areas and much more on what members are doing 'out there' For example, the Church of Scotland's first full-time industrial chaplain, the Revd Cameron Wallace, working in the shipyards on the lower reaches of the Clyde, reported on what he felt to be the Church's inadequacy in the industrial field:

> It would be difficult to deny the dichotomy between life in society and life in industry. This poses the Church with a bitter dilemma, unless it further retreats and accepts the position already assigned to it by many as an exclusive ecclesiastical club for the religiously minded. The fact is that the Church, through its members, is deeply entrenched in every stratum of industry, but is woefully ineffective.

Cameron Wallace's pioneering work in helping Christians to reflect on their responsibilities at the workplace paved the way for experiments elsewhere.

Many new members joined the Community not to work in urban Scotland, but to go overseas — to Pakistan, South Africa, Kenya, Northern Rhodesia, Nigeria, Nyasaland, India, Gibraltar, the USA, Canada — bringing to the Community many insights and questions.

Lindesay Robertson, an engineer, went to Nyasaland to work on a local village development scheme, and stayed for thirty years. He reported back to his Iona brethren:

> The idea is to retain as much as possible of the old village culture, but at the same time to create an economic structure which makes it possible for the village to undertake projects to develop its own life and industry . . . we are very lucky here in that we have this village, close by the mission on what used to be mission land. We have a wonderful opportunity

here of evolving a Christian way of life for a village
community, and at the same time of supplying much
needed technical assistance and guidance.

A remarkable experiment in community in India was made by
two Iona members and their wives — George and Mary More and
David and Alison Lyon. They went to live in the village of Allipur
with an Indian pastor and his wife. They sold the mission bungalow
and bought a small field beside the village on which they built
accommodation for guests and small conferences. They shared
salaries and tasks as they searched for a pattern of closer community
living. George wrote:

> This local community does not solve other people's
> problems but a community which is learning to
> reconcile British and Indian in common meals, service
> and worship, with families so different in income,
> may open a way for others. We do it because it is our
> obedience, our salvation, our joy.

George and Mary lived there for thirty years and continued to
look to the Iona Community for inspiration. Their experience in
India compelled them to raise difficult questions for the Church in
Scotland, and to challenge the Iona Community:

> In responding to all the new insight being given to
> us in India about unity, community and the local
> church, the life of Scotland and its Church is of highly
> dubious value. By the great luxury and riches of the
> Scottish people (and other Westerners) and by the
> methods of the Church of Scotland which acquiesce
> in that wealth, our Indian not-too-experienced second
> and third generation Christian leaders are too often
> perverted. The rich churches of the West have
> assumed, as of right, leadership in the World Council
> of Churches, without examining the effect of riches
> on the missionary movement. The Church of
> Scotland's own standard of living and assumption of
> leadership (shared by her foreign missionaries) has
> been one factor in the failure to produce an able and
> adequate indigenous ministry in the Eastern
> churches, thus weakening them in their

understanding of God and in their development and witness.

The thrust of George and Mary's message from India was that when they looked at the Church of Scotland, they did not see people similarly engaged in the same mission. What they saw were people busily engaged in maintaining religious institutions.

The Revd David Orr, minister of Govan Old Parish church, reflected on this in the light of his nine years' ministry in Fife. Too much effort went into maintaining the institution, he said, while groups set up to deal with issues of life were ignored.

> If they pack up, nobody cares; this is incidental. Christian Aid Weeks, Refugee Years, nuclear disarmament campaigns, African issues — things which might conceivably bear some relation to our unity in Christ; well, it's only those of us who are particularly resilient and thick-skinned who can face the continual strain of raising such issues. The Church (by and large, except for a few) just isn't interested; or when they are accepted as part of the job of the Church they're far down on the agenda, and given the fag-end of our energy, and of our planning, and of our money.

David reported that in the midst of this two things inspired him: the growth of house churches, where the word was shared in people's homes, and the development of a corporate sacramental liturgy which enabled community to be seen around the holy table.

The life of the Iona Community was further enriched and disturbed by the witness and challenge of the considerable number of members who went to work in Africa. Church of Scotland missionaries were credited with considerable influence in the break-up of the iniquitous Central African Federation, and Iona men had their part to play in that. During his Moderatorial year, George MacLeod went to central Africa, and his passionate plea at the General Assembly of the Church of Scotland for justice for all Africans was part of a witness of which the Kirk can justly be proud.

Community members found themselves compelled to speak up against oppression in Africa wherever they found it. Andrew Ross and Albert McAdam were shown the door by the government of

Malawi, and Graeme Brown, one of a number of Community members involved in protest against apartheid, was not allowed to return to his post as principal of a theological college in South Africa.

The African dimension of the Community's work was further enriched by way of music. Tom Colvin collected words and music from Malawi, and they made their way into the songbooks of the world Church via Iona Abbey.

Back home in Scotland, Community men continued to beaver away in parishes and communities, seeking to forge links between worship and radical political and social action. The work was always controversial: ministers who were known to be members of the Iona Community often found obstacles when they sought a new charge. Radical motions about Africa or domestic politics were often regarded on the floor of the General Assembly of the Church of Scotland as part of a sinister Jesuitical conspiracy.

Two members of Community, Walter Fyfe and John Jardine, joined with a third colleague, Geoff Shaw, to establish a community in the notorious Gorbals district of Glasgow. It was inspired by East Harlem Protestant Parish, New York, which in turn had been influenced by George MacLeod and the Iona experiment, and was written up by another Community member, Bruce Kenrick, in his influential book *Come out the Wilderness*. The three men initiated a life of sharing, worship, caring and political action, and the Gorbals Group went on to make a significant witness.

Another radical experiment strongly influenced by the Iona Community was the establishment of a 'Factory for Peace', run without share capital on a co-operative basis. The light engineering company produced goods in Glasgow, with all profits to be used for peace. Called 'Rowen Engineering' after Robert Owen's pioneering project at New Lanark, it was an attempt to find a new model of partnership in industrial relations. It lasted for a few years under the leadership of Tom McAlpine, with much of the support coming from Iona members and sympathizers, but eventually ran into economic difficulty. Jim Hughes and David Jarvie, Community members engaged in industry, continued to pioneer new methods of running industrial concerns.

On Iona, the numbers of students, pilgrims and tourists increased. The laying of electric cables under the Sound of Iona meant that the season lasted longer, and the introduction of a car ferry from

Oban to Mull helped swell the number of day visitors. The demand for summer conferences continued, and leaders such as Sir Richard Acland, H. H. Farmer, F. C. Happold, Frank Lake, R. D. Laing, Hugh Montefiore, Martin Niemöller, Ronald Gregor Smith, Paul Oestreicher and John Vincent counted it a privilege to teach on Iona for a week.

Perhaps the most vital work of all was done in the youth camps, where young people from the Gorbals, Bridgeton, London, Liverpool, Germany, Holland and the USA met together for worship, discussion, recreation and social activity. What was on offer was neither trendy nor cheap, but the vitality of worship in the Abbey church both invigorated and challenged all who participated.

John Jardine, while youth secretary, wrote:

> From many lands, of different colours, with great variety in social background, education and daily work, men and women, they eat, work, talk, play and worship together. Seldom a week passes without one or two campers coming from outwith the British Isles, from other parts of Europe, across the Atlantic, from several African countries, India, Australia, New Zealand. Scarcely less varied are the remainder of the campers. Coming from as far apart as Inverness, Donegal, Norfolk, and Cornwall, accents differ as much as occupations. In recent summers a pattern has been maintained.
>
> Rough figures are twenty-two per cent industrial workers, seven per cent technical and laboratory assistants, thirty per cent office workers, nineteen per cent students, five per cent shop workers, ten per cent in professions, with the remainder less easy to classify but adding no less to the richness of camp life . . .
>
> At a time when not for many years has the Community been so concerned about the pattern of its life we might do well to consider if some of the signs of the sought-for pattern are not already present in the life of the youth camps. Christ Himself pointed

out that the kingdom of God belongs to children, and this rather prodigious child — some five to six hundred young people come to camp each summer — is something for which the Iona Community carries sole responsibility. The small groups of young workers brought by the Christian Workers League to camp in Iona in the last summers of the war could hardly have known that they were the beginning of an enterprise which has brought over four thousand young people to spend a week in camp in just over a decade. Nor is it probable that the Community itself realized what it was starting.

The 1950s and 60s represented a time of extraordinary vitality, growth and creativity in the life of the Iona Community. Perhaps it was the sound of the beating of wings which muffled the steady but insistent questions which ticked away quietly like a time bomb.

8

The End of the Beginning?

When Dr Eammon de Valera, Taoiseach (Prime Minister) of Eire, came unannounced to Iona for a visit, he was shown round the Abbey by Dr MacLeod. The Iona leader remembered the visit:

> I attempted to be his guide, not a little embarrassed by the presence of his son, an expert in the High Crosses of Ireland. He courteously corrected me three times in my description of our own. The Premier was charm itself, truly catholic in generous congratulation of our building purpose, but even more delighted by the singing of God's praise upon which he had stumbled, when he had expected to enter an empty dismal fane. I was, he said, to return with him for luncheon on the Corsair, but we were a vigorous community with a closeknit programme, and I begged to be excused. 'Then, when you next visit Dublin,' he almost commanded, 'you will by my guest.'
>
> 'Is there anything I can do for you?' he asked as we passed St Martin's Cross on his departure. He had been so whimsical that I dared an impertinence. 'You can return to us the Book of Kells from Trinity College, Dublin, for was it not wrought here?'

I saw across his brow a gathering furrow, such as Lloyd George must have known when Republican conversations were at their worst, so I hastily added, 'Of course, you could take away St Martin's Cross in part exchange.' Calm returned to his brow. 'You can have the Book of Kells for nothing, on one condition — that you bring Iona within the hegemony of the Irish Free State.'

'Not on your life, sir', I replied, and he renewed his invitation that I return to Dublin.

When George MacLeod became Moderator and paid a visit to Dublin, he took the Taoiseach at his word.

I wrote ahead and suggested I call on him for a cup of coffee in the Dáil. But nothing less would satisfy him than an official state luncheon. The hospitality was lavish. Knowing a speech lay before me, I was content with a simple sherry. Other Scottish delegates were able to enter more, shall we say, into the spirit of the party.

During one of those pauses that speak louder than words, the entire table could do no other than hear, only too distinctly, a Scottish delegate ask, 'What, Mr Prime Minister, would you say is the main difference between Northern and Southern Ireland?' During the instantaneous and yet immemorial pause that followed this innocent but outrageous sally, a distinct swish was heard outside the window. It was the Liffey turning back on its flow. By way of desperate remedy I almost shouted, 'Would you ever consider sailing in a curragh with me, sir, from Derry to Iona when we all celebrate the fourteenth centenary of the arrival of St Columba?' The situation was saved as the Premier discoursed most learnedly on the building of curraghs then and now. I assured him I was in earnest, and promised that a friend of mine with a modern yacht could sail in our wake and make transfer possible in the event of a storm.

'Bring your yacht,' he countered, 'but she can sail
ahead of the coracle. In any storm they could transfer
to our craft!'

The conversation was not entirely in vain. During the fourteenth-
centenary celebrations, the planning of which caused so much
excitement, a coracle made the trip, safely, from Ireland to Iona.

The fellowship of the Iona Community continued to grow through
plenaries and family groups. Plenary meetings of all members who
could attend were held on Iona and the mainland. They were marked
by robust debate about the issues facing the Church, but also by a
sharing of personal concerns. Members working in different parts of
the country rejoiced to meet together and share a common vocabulary
of faith.

To return to Iona with fellow members and stand in the Abbey
church for the familiar responses of the morning service — "Except
the Lord build the house, they labour in vain that build it" — felt
like coming back home. Meeting together for worship and discussion
gave members a renewed vision for their often difficult work, and
sharing in the annual Hallowing Service, at which new members
were dedicated and all the overseas members were prayed for by
name, reinforced the sense of solidarity and mutual support.

This support was further strengthened at regional family groups.
Members and their wives met together regularly in each others'
homes to participate in the Iona Community liturgy, go over the
disciplines of the Community and share matters of common interest.
Nor were family groups all-Scottish affairs. For instance, nine
members and their spouses in India met together for a week at
Nagpur, Bombay State. Each day began with the Community office
and finished with family prayers. Discussions were held on the task
of the Church in India and what it meant to be a member of the
Iona Community in Asia. At the end of the week, the members
reported to the wider Iona Community:

> The thing that counted most in this week was
> belonging to one another in community where there
> was complete trust and acceptance. The group was
> pastoral and healing, and we needed both. The fact
> that it was a family group enriched the experience
> beyond measure . . . we were all of us during this

week very much aware of our unity with members of
the Community in Scotland.

As the fourteenth-centenary celebrations of the coming of Columba
to Iona drew nearer, the insistent questions became less muffled:
What was to be done with the Abbey when the buildings were
complete, and what would happen to the Iona Community?

In 1956 George MacLeod had suggested that when the buildings
were complete, a way might open up for an agricultural community
to be developed for intensive market gardening, or co-operating with
the farmers of Iona in the urgent problem of West Highland recovery.
Not many members of his Community agreed with him.

MacLeod felt that the situation had changed somewhat since the
foundation of the Community — yet there was still a need for it. He
argued that many of the issues that used to concern the Iona
Community were now the common concerns of the whole Church.
Mission, divine healing, political concern, trade union involvement
and liturgical reform were all accepted — though not by any means
due to the work of the Iona Community alone.

> It may be that the Iona Community, by its smallness,
> was able to make quicker and more observable thrusts
> in all these fields (he wrote), but in themselves these
> activities no longer give reason for our separate
> existence.

> But there is a discernment that has arisen from our
> experiments, which we do not yet find has common
> acceptance in the general body of the Church. It is
> that 'unless all these interests hang together they will
> all hang separately'. In short, you dare not merely
> pray for direct divine healing for one with TB if you
> know it was contracted in the Gorbals of Glasgow.
> You must add to your prayer direct political action
> in the matter of Gorbals housing: nor can you do
> anything at all about the housing of the Gorbals
> except by party political action. Thus healing and
> politics hang together. Thus, also, we will not solve
> the political problems of our time unless we recover
> the social significance of the sacrament. Our greatest
> world problem is how to share bread: yet the

sacrament of Holy Communion is just such sharing though it is not many politicians who so see politics . . . our bread will go bad in the fields, on the Exchanges and on our Communion tables until we recover the nexus and see all these issues together as contemporaneous mission.

It remains highly important, then, that we have a Community whose centre remains in Iona, to declare, with its hands, its head and its heart that One Body of concern that is the unique challenge of the Christian faith. To this it can only bear witness in an Abbey that adjoins an eating place where the discussion is all embracing.

So the Iona leader saw the primary role of his Community in the future as being a living reminder to the Church of its need to preach and live a total gospel in which prayer and political work for justice were sides of the same coin. But he also saw Iona having a special role in the areas of ecumenical relationships, international justice and personal holiness.

Certainly it is true in our unified world, that if the denominations do not hang together they will hang separately. But there is no subject about which so much can be wisely written and carefully not done as Church unity! The world is dying for the lack of the reconciling Word. Constantly we prate, 'if only all nations were Christians they would unite'. But why should they be interested in becoming Christian — as the proffered uniting agency — when the churches themselves cannot unite! South Africa is most in need of reconciliation — Christian reconciliation. How terrible then that there are two hundred and forty registered denominations of Christianity in South Africa. We may have the word 'on paper' but until we are the word, men will not listen, nor should they.

Some of us in the Community believe that it was no accident that the eighth Duke of Argyll expressed

the hope, when he returned the Abbey to the Church
of Scotland, that all denominations might worship
there, each according to its fullest rite. May Iona
become an ecumenical centre of Church unity?

On the subject of international justice, MacLeod argued that
charity was not enough.

It is clear enough the issue will not be served by
voluntary effort — a food ship there, seed to the next
place, and tractors to a third. Ambulances are
necessary but they never win battles. Global political
action is required. But there is no global political
action save through the tedious process of dismal
party politics. Some of us in the Community believe
that, while the General Church now champions the
necessity of political involvement, a focal centre is
wanted of the supreme political issue as it challenges
churchmen — the issue of war on want, politically
and not just amelioratively conceived.

Some of us in the Community believe that it was no
accident that brought us to the centre of the old Celtic
tradition. For the first missionaries who went out
from there carried not only a book, a bell and a staff.
Each also carried a bag of seed. Christ was the total
Bread of Life. May Iona become an ecumenical centre
of Bread Politics?

Calling for a new way of holiness which took the personal and the
corporate equally seriously, MacLeod concluded :

Only Christ can save us now, body and soul:
politically and ecclesiastically. All that is implied in
this dual nexus has not been faced by the Church for
over sixteen hundred years. May Iona become an
ecumenical centre for the new holiness — personal
as well as corporate!

'In Iona,' said St Columba, 'God will reveal Himself
anew.' We cannot know what this means. Certainly
no man or movement could assist by one iota such a

revelation. But men can build cradles . . . Perhaps
the Iona Community, in these immediate years, is
not completing a task but being made aware that it
may have a home now from which to begin for the
first time — to fashion cradles.

It is interesting that in this first major rethink of the Community's
purpose since 1938, urban Scotland is hardly mentioned. The feeling
appears to be that the initial purpose of the Community has been
taken over by the mainstream churches, and it is now time for the
Community to address itself to other concerns. The emphasis in
The Coracle moves to issues: peace, Third World poverty and injustice,
and African affairs. Two Associates making a return visit to Iona
wrote, more in sadness than in anger, to complain that the
Community was no longer dealing in specifics, and had lost direction.

The rebuilding went on apace, as money continued to come in.
Work on the abbot's house, the cloisters, St Michael's chapel and
the West Range pointed towards the finished product. Was the Iona
Community a finished product as well — one whose purpose was
nearing completion?

Asking whether it was the beginning of the end or the end of the
beginning, Ralph Morton asserted:

'The Community has to make many decisions. The
rebuilding on Iona is nearly finished. And we are so
used to that work of rebuilding as giving the
background of the Community's life, that it's hard
to awaken to the fact that we must find another. The
door is open — to strange possibilities and great
demands.'

While the questioning about fundamentals was going on privately,
the visitors and pilgrims continued to head for the inspiring
Hebridean island. The directors of the major European laity centres
came to Iona to confer and were enchanted by the community
emphasis of the set-up, as well as by the history and beauty of the
island.

To meet the demand for information, the Community published
What is the Iona Community? and *The Iona Community Story*. The
Community was now old enough to have a history to tell and retell
and even a Golden Age, whose passing the greybeards could lament.

Pentecost 1963 was not a time for lamentations, however. The fourteen hundredth anniversary of the time Columba set foot on Iona was a time of great celebration and story telling. Gifts were dedicated: a figure of St Michael, an amplification system for Abbey worship, a staff, bible and replica of a sixth-century Celtic handbell for St Columba's shrine, a beautifully carved lectern to stand between the Abbey sanctuary and choir in the original medieval socket, and lighting accessories to allow St Columba's shrine, the North Transept, the Michael Chapel and the west door of the Abbey to be lit and welcoming long after dark.

On Pentecost Sunday, Holy Communion was celebrated by Bishop Lesslie Newbigin — a Scots Presbyterian who was also a bishop of the Church of South India. The preacher was the Rt Revd Professor James S. Stewart, Moderator of the General Assembly of the Church of Scotland, who was one of the original sponsors of the Iona Community. The major churches of Scotland were represented, with the exception of the Roman Catholic Church. Guests included Brother Christopher from the Taizé Community in France, with which the Iona Community had close links, and Father Vladimir Rodzianko of the Greek Orthodox Church.

On St Columba's Day, 9 June, over a thousand pilgrims (only a proportion of those who applied to come) came by land and sea to a special ceremony of dedication. They were led by young people along the recently excavated Street of the Dead towards St Columba's shrine for a simple act of personal dedication. Down at the jetty, the Moderator of the Presbyterian Church in Ireland handed over the gift of a Donegal fishing boat, the *Derry*, to allow the young Iona campers to sail to places such as Camas and Erraid of *Kidnapped* fame.

When Columba and his followers arrived in Iona in 563, the news took some time to get around. Fourteen hundred years later, the celebrations of the saint's arrival were conveyed throughout Britain and six European countries by means of television. George MacLeod recalled a strange experience which was not recorded by the all-seeing eye.

> Immediately prior to the commencement of the celebrations, I had naturally been very busy with a host of details to be co-ordinated. When dawn broke on Sunday 2nd June, I woke considerably surprised

to feel not an atom of tiredness in my being. Knowing the pressures of the coming day I got up at six with the intention of getting on top of the day before events began to crowd in on one another. As I was dressing I was conscious of a strong wind, alternately moaning and almost whistling through the house. I looked out to sea, which seemed calm. I looked at nearby trees which seemed still. I then saw the carpet rippling up and down. I woke my wife who, not unreasonably, suggested that someone must have left the front door or a large window open. I examined all doors and windows and returned and again shut the door of the room, but the carpet was still rippling like a moving yet somehow static snake. The wind also continued.

As I crossed towards the Abbey I was still aware of the wind which somehow was not yet blowing me about. And into my mind came Pentecost with its 'sound of the rushing mighty wind, and it filled all the house where they were sitting'. This biblical language precisely described my immediate experiences.

On becoming thus aware of a modern Pentecost I immediately began to wonder whether I was becoming slightly light-headed, with all that had been going on late into the night before and so early in the morning. Was I definitely 'air borne'? — I asked myself — and would I do something silly in the course of the day? That gave way (I still had not covered the few hundred yards to the west door of the Abbey) to the question in myself whether I ever expect anything really overtly spiritual to happen? Do you get me?

If hundreds of people come to Iona on Pentecost determined to partake of the sacrament together the whole Church — for the first time for centuries, if they have all been praying for a great day, is it really extraordinary that something should happen? As

Christians in our modern world, are we really expecting ANYTHING to happen?

Other winds were blowing on Iona.

Laymen in the Community were asking: When the Abbey buildings are completed, will they be taken over by ministers for their concerns?

Ministers were asking: Have we not, in our diversity, departed too much from the original intentions of the Community?

Women were asking: Why is it that we can come to youth camps on Iona, but not live in the Abbey or be full members of the Community? Is this so-called radical community not just a male clerical club?

Increasing numbers of members were asking: Are we not too dependent on one man and his views? If we are truly a community, should we not be more corporate in our decision-making?

Insiders and outsiders were asking: Is the Community not becoming too big? Should we not draw the line at eighty members and allow no more admissions?

Good, honest rebellion was in the air. It was generally acknowledged that the Community attracted many able men in the Church of Scotland and they were not short of the odd word or two. The higher the Community's profile, the more able people sought to join and the more diverse it became. This led in turn to more passionate debate and argument. The temper of the times was for increased democracy and participation, and George MacLeod was given a harder ride. The leader, in turn, was impatient with blethering and wanted more decisive action.

There is a story in the Community's folklore that George decided that more democracy was perhaps in order. A new carpet was to be laid in one of the main rooms. George wanted a red one, so the Community, flexing its muscles, voted for a green one. The members left the island feeling satisfied! The new carpet was duly laid. It was red.

At Pentecost 1965 the West Range was dedicated, effectively bringing to conclusion the superb restoration of Iona Abbey buildings. The great door to the West Range was opened by David Russell chairman of the Iona Appeal Trust, who with his father Sir David Russell had done so much to encourage and support the rebuilding and the excavations of the historical sites. Some eight hundred attended an open-air Communion facing towards the Abbey from Tor Abb (the excavated cell of Columba) and centred on Columba's restored shrine. Within the shrine itself, a perpetual light was lit — a beacon used by ships coming up from the south. After the televised service, the worshippers moved into the newly restored cloisters, where they were asked to share a piece of the consecrated loaf with someone they had never met before — a custom believed to go back to the Celtic Church. With representatives of sixteen nations present, the occasion was truly Pentecostal.

Although various bits of work continued for a further two years, the main task was over. It had been exhilarating and exhausting — a common task which had released the talents of many and whose symbolism had inspired people throughout the world. The restored Abbey, with its simplicity of line, West Highland strength and dignity and Hebridean beauty enabled the final part of the Columban prophecy to be added:

> In Iona of my heart, Iona of my love,
> Instead of monks' voices shall be lowing of cattle;
> But 'ere the world come to an end,
> Iona shall be as it was.

9

The Shaking of the Foundations

When it came it was a great shock, even to the members of the Iona Community. Like everyone else, they first learned of it from the newspapers: George MacLeod had been elevated to the peerage in the 1967 New Years Honours List, on the recommendation of the Labour Prime Minister, Mr Harold Wilson.

Furthermore, he was resigning as leader of the Iona Community.

It was hard enough to get used to the title, the Very Revd Lord MacLeod of Fuinary (the MacLeod family home in Morvern); to do without the leadership of the founder and creator of their movement represented a critical change. George MacLeod had nursed, challenged, charmed, bullied and inspired his Community for nearly thirty years. Latterly some had rebelled against his style of leadership — but when adolescent rebellion is followed by parental departure, all kinds of feelings are evoked. Thus at a time when the internationally applauded rebuilding of Iona Abbey was complete and the Community was agonizing about its role, its founder and mentor was moving on.

It was a time of crisis not just for the Iona Community, but for the Church as well. Cracks were appearing in the theological foundations, and familiar landmarks were disappearing. The optimistic post-war coalition, focused around the theology of Karl Barth, was breaking up. The 'Tell Scotland' movement, which had begun so promisingly, had, against opposition (including that of the Iona Community), elected to go the Billy Graham route — and what might have been a broadly based mission movement in Scotland became a vehicle for personal evangelism, American style.

The widespread circulation of Bishop John A. T. Robinson's paperback, *Honest to God*, helped to change the ethos of much church life in Britain. God, argued the Bishop, was not to be found 'out there' but in the depths. The picture of God presented by the mainstream churches, he suggested, was obsolete and needed to be completely redrawn.

This articulate polemic against traditional Christianity by a bishop of the Church was welcomed as a liberation by many people. Robinson drew on the work of two main theologians. Dietrich Bonhoeffer, who was martyred in a German prison during the Second World War, had argued in his *Letters and Papers from Prison* for what he termed 'religionless Christianity' — a form of faith based less on traditional religious observance than on inward discipleship in the world. For 'Man come of Age', he said, the old expressions of Christianity would not do. Paul Tillich, the American theologian, talked about 'the Ground of Being' rather than the God of traditional revealed religion, and described what was happening in theology as 'the shaking of the foundations'.

Robinson's somewhat half-baked summary of these ideas — for instance, he did much less than justice to Bonhoeffer's profound commitment to spiritual discipline and community — struck many chords. There had been a comprehensive change of ethos in Europe, best summed up in the current favourite word, 'secularization'. For many people, the traditional God was dead or, as the graffiti suggested, engaged on a less ambitious project. Was the Iona Community now engaged on a less ambitious project as well? It was certainly in a state of crisis, even though the extent of it was not fully realized at the time. The Community had been reared on confident assumptions about the Gospel and the Church. George MacLeod's angle was that a reformed Church which truly lived the Gospel would draw people like a magnet, even in the poorest areas. The quickest and most effective route to that reform was a new training for ministers in community. The Gospel itself was not questioned: what George MacLeod and the Iona Community wanted to do was to seek out and live the radical implications of the biblical message.

The sea change of the 1960s put everything under question. That heady blend of scientific progress, economic growth, idealism, honesty, consumerism, swinging lifestyles, humbug and exploitation made the Church look like a moralizing dinosaur. People seeking progress and justice looked not to the Church but to the civil rights movements and the political systems.

As elsewhere in Europe, the Church in Scotland suffered a slump in numbers and a steady erosion of confidence in its message and organization. Even Christian thinkers began to see the Church as an obstacle to progress and despaired of its renewal. Ministers, themselves afflicted by doubts, found themselves presiding over shrinking congregations of anxious people determined to defend the ramparts. It was a confusing and frustrating situation, and many able people left the ministry to live in what was felt to be the 'real' world, rather than continue to inhabit a defensive ecclesiastical ghetto.

Iona Community ministers experienced the cold draught, even in the new housing areas and new towns. Stewart McGregor, a minister in the new town of Cumbernauld, told of how easy it was for a congregation to turn in on itself and become a religious club for the few. At one church, he said, an elder had suggested turning a cold hose on the boisterous youth club! He wrote:

> If the Church is for others it would take us quite a long time to discover it. In the present pattern of our church life, in organizations, in financial appeals, in our attitude to the life of the member inside and to the life of the world outside, and even in the structures of our worship, the content of our prayers and the choice of our hymns, are we in the Church not guilty of committing, as a community, those very sins which we are so ready to deplore in individuals: the sins of selfishness, self-centredness, self-importance, acquisitiveness and lack of concern for others?

Gordon Strachan talked about his training on Iona, then meeting the reality of life in an Edinburgh housing scheme parish:

> It was a good transition period from college to parish, stimulating and provoking. The community life and

magic of the island went admirably together. We caught the tang of fresh winds, other minds, and from the start were given great hospitality, a sense of belonging. The whole conception of life on the island bore the stamp of an imaginative approach to religion.

In West Pilton, he found that only three per cent of the community were active in the church.

The unchurched majority make contact with the Church mainly through births, marriages and deaths. In an interview a mother asking for her child's baptism may reveal that she has not heard of Jesus or His death.

It was in the face of such problems and questions that the Iona Community had to reshape its vocation at the end of the time of rebuilding. George MacLeod had attempted just such a reshaping a year before his retirement as leader. Again, it is significant that wider issues replace urban Scotland as the main focus. The building in which the Iona Community is now engaged is inward rather than outward, MacLeod said, and pointing out that the old bastions were collapsing, he wrote that:

We must pause to consider where we stand in all this 'honest to God' mood. The future significance of the Iona Community depends not on its intellectual interpretation of the present situation, but on what action it takes in and through that interpretation. It is where it stands that will enlighten what it thinks.

Amidst the crumbling, Dr MacLeod saw signs of hope. Einstein had said that there was no such thing as dead matter — the ultimate form of matter was light-energy. Science was moving away from purely intellectual knowledge towards a deeper knowledge that was more compatible with faith. What was needed was a new reformation which would bond together the spiritual and the material.

Suppose the material order, as we have argued, is indeed the garment of Christ, the temple of the Holy Ghost? Suppose the bread and wine, symbols of all creation, is indeed capable of redemption awaiting its Christification? Then what is the atom but the emergent body of Christ?

The Feast of the Transfiguration is 6th August. That is the day we 'happened' to drop the bomb on Hiroshima. We took His Body and we took His Blood and we enacted a Cosmic Golgotha. We took the key to love and we used it for bloody hell.

Nobody noticed. I am not being cheap about other people. I did not notice it myself. I was celebrating the Feast of the Transfiguration in a gown and a cassock, a hood, a stole, white bands, saying with the whole Christian ministry, 'This is my body, this is my blood'. The while our 'Christian civilization', without Church protest, made its assertion of the complete divorce between Spirit and Matter.

Saying that non-violence and international monetary policy were two key areas for a Church which believed in the unity of the spiritual and the material, he added, 'Iona can be the home of the New Reformation. But it must recover its genius: keep acting its insights at whatever risk if its insights are to be clarified and the next obedience seen.'

George MacLeod argued within the Community that Iona Abbey should become a new faculty for the training of theological students in Scotland. He lost the argument, the majority believing that to use the Abbey for professional training was to turn back the clock and be too restrictive.

It was agreed that, with the completion of the rebuilding, the initial training for new minister members should be changed — the first part of the time would be spent on Iona and the second part living as a team in Community House, Glasgow, while working outside. The Abbey would 'continue and develop as a place of meeting, conference and training'.

Issues continued to dominate the life of the Community. Peace was one of the key concerns, and in 1966 the debates resulted in the adoption of an Act of Commitment on peace as part of the Rule of the Community. The preamble in the original version read:

It is a solemn undertaking. It is our point of departure and not of arrival. It is our vow rather than our view. It is the first time that the Community has come to an agreed statement on a political topic. Previously the Community has expressed unanimous concern on certain subjects but left it to members to decide their own line of action. It has taken its place as part of the commitment of membership, as serious as devotional discipline. And it is a commitment to action. It must be implemented in detailed individual and communal action.

The Act of Commitment went on:

1. We believe that peacemaking is integral to the Gospel.

2. We believe that in the present time international peacemaking is of unprecedented urgency and requires a massive effort.

3. We believe that racial discrimination and the ever-widening economic gap between the over-developed and the developing nations are major causes of international tension and conflict.

4. We believe that the use of nuclear and other weapons of mass destruction is morally indefensible even by the standards of 'the just war' and politically ineffective as an instrument of policy, and that the attempt to maintain peace by their threats is dangerous and undesirable.

5. We undertake to do everything in our power to make discussion, prayer and action about international peace an important part of the life of the Church at all levels.

6. We undertake to work for the establishment of the United Nations as the principal organ of international integration and security, replacing military alliances.

7.   We undertake to work for the closing of the
     economic gap between the over-developed and the
     developing nations.

8.   We undertake to work for a British policy of
     renunciation of all weapons of mass destruction
     and promotion of their effective control by the
     United Nations, aimed at their limitation,
     reduction and removal.

9.   We undertake to work for the support and
     establishment of peace research centres.

10. We undertake to promote and, where possible,
     participate in large-scale international sharing and
     exchange of personnel and experience as, for
     example, through visits, short-term service and
     long-term employment, paying special attention
     to exchange with communist and developing
     nations.

The Peace Commitment was something of a compromise. Most of
the Community favoured unilateral nuclear disarmament, but some,
including Ian Reid, supported nuclear disarmament by Britain but
not immediately by the West — implying, if necessary, continuing
American nuclear bases in Britain. The Peace Commitment
represented an attempt to take both positions into account while
making a positive statement about peacemaking.

The Rule of the Iona Community was increasingly important in
binding together members in different jobs in different parts of the
world. It was now a five-point Rule — a commitment to prayer,
economic sharing, planning of time, meeting together and
peacemaking.

Members were still, of course, involved in reform and experiment.
The house church movement was one of the livelier parts of the
Church's life, and Community members were much involved in it,
both in terms of organization and writing. And members were still
concerned to shape 'cradles' of new life and experiment.

James Maitland, a former warden of Community House, was
appointed by the Church of Scotland to help pioneer an ecumenical
experiment in the new town of Livingston. He said that he and his

two colleagues had no blueprint for the experiment, but they shared some deeply-held convictions:

> That there is a power in the Gospel of the Kingdom to rescue men from the divisiveness of class, culture and religion. That God means His Church to live and work and worship as one people. That in our day only a servant Church can communicate a saving Gospel. That the Church's primary ministry belongs to the laity, and the main job of the professional ministry is to help the laity recognize and answer its calling to be the Church scattered in every department of secular life.

In Sheffield, Donald McIlhagga was appointed minister of a new united Presbyterian-Congregational church. Another 'cradle' had been fashioned by Bruce Kenrick in multiracial Notting Hill — his pioneering work in the field of housing led directly to the formation of Shelter, which has done so much for homeless people in Britain.

Community men were also involved in various forms of specialist ministry and chaplaincy work, particularly in industry and education.

The Iona experiment was influential in other ways. The founding of the Corrymeela Community by Ray Davey owed much to the inspiration of Iona. Corrymeela went on to develop its outstanding role as a reconciling influence between Protestants and Roman Catholics in battle-torn Northern Ireland, and John Morrow, who succeeded Ray Davey leader of the Corrymeela Community, was himself an Iona member. The New Harmony community in Indiana also owed much to the inspiration of the Iona experiment.

Community House in Glasgow continued to play an important role in the life of the West of Scotland, though its outreach work diminished when the Lithgow funding ceased. The House was handed over to the Community and the caring and educational work continued, though the Community had to engage in ceaseless efforts to raise the necessary funds.

The Iona Community was faced, for the first time in its history, with the election of a new leader. Ralph Morton stepped down as deputy leader. It was the end of a long and fruitful, if sometimes fraught, partnership. George MacLeod acknowledged, in a tribute to Ralph, 'I think it is true that in recent years his interpretation of our times has increasingly differed from my own.' The two different styles and approaches had contributed so much to the growth and development of the Iona movement.

Ian Reid, minister of the Old Kirk, Pilton, was elected to undertake the onerous task of filling George MacLeod's shoes and took up office in September 1967. He acknowledged the realities of a Community which no longer had a unified, confident view of the Church:

> The Community exists to help its members together to receive both vision and encouragement. At the present time there are those who, in obedience to Jesus, feel dissatisfied with the institutional Church as it is. Some of them know that they must remain within the institutional Church trying to help it to become the kind of Church He wants. Others, still committed to Jesus, believe that they must work outside it. These two groups need one another.

10

The Long Haul

There came a time in the life of the Early Church when the realization dawned that a revised, less certain, timetable would have to be drawn up for the longed-for return of Jesus Christ. As second- and third-generation Christians died out, the script had to be rewritten and the Church's provisional, apocalyptic organization had to give way to something more suited to the long and dusty road ahead.

Though hardly of the same magnitude, a similar kind of problem confronted the Iona Community. Its rebuilding project was complete, its founder and his deputy had retired, the revolution had not come and the Community had not disbanded itself. It was to Ian Reid's credit that he grasped the nettle. A conscientious pastor and tireless worker, the new leader provided an organizational structure for the next stage of the Community's life. A treasurer was appointed and the finances were established on a firmer footing. The committee structure encouraged more responsibility by members.

It was a difficult time in which to lead the Iona movement. The ferment of questioning in the Church generally, allied to the incessant debating about the role of the Iona Community after the rebuilding, meant that Ian Reid's role was an exacting and sometimes thankless one. The glamour which attaches to a new and exciting radical movement had faded, and the new leader had to rely on persuasion rather than on stunning eloquence or charismatic brilliance.

He had a hard act to follow — or even to live alongside. George MacLeod remained a member of the Iona Community, yet although he now had no executive position within the Community, he was hardly a back-bencher. And he found it hard to let go. Never a lover of committees, this man of restless energy grew impatient with talk. As one who never doubted the Gospel or the importance of the Church, he was not enamoured of endless debate about such matters. Ian Reid bore the murmurings and pressure of his distinguished predecessor with fortitude and grace.

George MacLeod's restlessness can be seen in his activities. In 1969, he was elected Rector of Glasgow University. In the same year he launched 'The New Breakthrough in Christ' — designed to mobilize people committed to a pacifist interpretation of Christian faith. His pamphlet, *An Idea Whose Hour is Come*, was a typical MacLeodian mixture of passionate rhetoric, romantic history, uncritical treatment of Scripture, and moving testimony. The launching of this new movement undoubtedly sprang from his annoyance at what he felt was the prevarication of the Iona Community on issues of peace and justice. He was keen that the Community should have a 'line' on these issues — a clear, agreed, radical stance. The Community's diversity in the midst of an ethos that favoured questions rather than answers ensured that their founder would become increasingly frustrated.

George MacLeod's obsession was with peace and he saw the Church's failure to speak clearly to the situation as a symptom of its loss of theological nerve.

> The Church today is paralysed with self-analysis. Its mission has become uncertain, its worship, still reverently respected, has lost its zest, even clergy discuss how far they are committed to prayer. From the pulpit the trumpet sounds with an uncertain voice. Bible reading has become a duty and not the daily necessity of the soul. Where the sociology classrooms are full, the divinity halls drop in numbers. In our four divinity halls together there is now one full-time professor or lecturer for every three of our regular students. We also are at our eleventh hour.
>
> Most assuredly it is not a new preoccupation with the things of peace that will revive us. The Bomb is

not God's trick to recover His institutional Church. But a faithful obedience to the Way of the Cross, for the twentieth century, can do no other than take account of our modern plight and see faithlessness as the cause of our secular world.

MacLeod poured much of his spare energy into the New Breakthrough in Christ, writing to people all over the country, asking them to sign up as supporters. Douglas Alexander, supporting the idea within the Community, wrote, 'At the moment it is more a Gesture than a Movement. It may indeed remain a Gesture whose true value lies in its power to evoke response rather than to evolve a structural pattern.' Despite its title, the New Breakthrough never really got beyond the stage of being a gesture.

Freed from the constraints of day-to-day responsibilities for the life of the Community, George MacLeod gave his attention to hammering out a new version of radical Christianity. The Church, he argued, had simply become part of the problem, with no word or life to set against the dominant secular trend. Christianity should present an alternative to worldly values, particularly from the vantage point of the cross of Christ.

At the General Assembly of the Church of Scotland, Lord MacLeod turned his attention to the international bankers who, he said, really ran the world and were sowing the seeds of the next world war. His vision was that of the Church taking on the bankers, but he feared that the Church was too tied in with the world to take any action whatsoever. The General Assembly declined to accept his plea to establish a committee to investigate the working of international finance.

What is clear is that George MacLeod's relationship with the Community he had founded and loved, and of which he was still a loyal member, was by the early 1970s a very mixed one indeed. The Community needed to grow to maturity without depending on a father figure, and some of the rejecting things of this stage were evidence of the need for elbowroom. Yet many of those who wanted more democracy, participation and consensus and felt it would do no harm for the trumpet to make a less than certain sound, felt the old goose pimples when the great man spoke and wondered whether he might not be right. George, on the other hand, was exasperated by the endless debates and analysis within the Community and his insistent pacifism became much more of a divisive issue than it had been. While the focus had been on the rebuilding of the Abbey and the training of clergy, pacifism had not been pushed and indeed had been deliberately played down: now that the Community was becoming more of an 'issues' movement, pacifism came more to the fore — and such was the force of George's personality that he who was not with him on this burning issue was against him. There was a danger of a group within the Community coalescing around the founder, making life difficult for the new leader.

Amidst all this turmoil, the Community continued to attract laymen to its membership, further changing the balance and interests. In 1969, Dr Nancy Brash, a former Church of Scotland medical missionary in North India, became the first woman to join the Iona Community. The male bastion had been breached.

For some, it was too much. The masculine regime of the early days had militated against the presence of women, as had the practical arrangements for the rebuilding. George MacLeod's concern to bring industrial men into the Church had also been a major shaping force in the style of the new Community. At the beginning, the Community was made up largely of unmarried men.

The invisibility of women has to be seen in the context of the general assumptions of the time. But after all the mitigating factors are heard, the judgement has to be made that the story of the Community's response to women does not constitute one of the more glorious chapters in its history. The Community's acceptance of women came only because women persisted. The setting up of Women's Associates was the first step, but the Community on Iona had remained a male preserve.

What really opened up the situation was the arrival of young people. The youth camps on Iona were mixed, reflecting the mainland youth clubs from which they had come. The young men and women shared together in community, involved in worship, chores, discussion, concerts and dances.

Full membership of the Community had been restricted to men, since the new intake each year consisted of theological students. The men lived on the island for three months, in the early days that was not a problem, as almost all the students were unmarried. The situation changed after the war, as more mature men studied for the ministry and the average age for marriage dropped. It meant that married men seeking membership of the Iona Community had to say farewell to wives and families for three months — a situation which caused unhappiness and sometimes bitterness. The 'island of women' had become a psychological, rather than a physical, space. It was 1970 before a new member's wife could stay with him throughout the training period on the island. Some spouses were deeply resentful of a Community which claimed the loyalty of the husband and with whom he discussed their own financial affairs. The situation was eased by the establishment of family groups in which spouses could participate.

The male orientation of the Community's worship and communications reflected uncritically much of the church and national culture of the time. This fact made it no less hurtful to women interested in deep involvement in Iona, especially in view of the Community's pioneering spirit in many other areas. Indeed the Church of Scotland, with its women ministers and elders, was ahead of the Iona Community in this area of human relationships.

As membership developed, it was noticeable that the number of members intending to go into the parish ministry was proportionately smaller. What were the reasons? The fact that the Community was no longer primarily a training scheme for ministers, that the divinity colleges had themselves adopted some of the Iona insights in their new training methods, that many of the Community's views on matters such as worship and industrial mission were now part of the mainstream of the Church, that the Community no longer had the glamour of youth and pioneering innovation, that it was concerned much more with issues which were seen to be divisive — all of these must have played their part.

With inevitable cutbacks in staffing, Community House also faced the problems of maintaining a dynamic role while being past the first exciting flush of youth. Television, which was hastening the demise of Sunday evening worship in many churches, was causing problems for voluntary organizations seeking to bring people in for educational classes. The post-war hunger for public discussion, training, drama and debate had steadily given way to more private concerns. Community House remained a base for west of Scotland activists and caring groups; the restaurant was a haven for many people and the warm acceptance provided by the House staff meant that alcoholics and down-and-outs spent much time there. Thus the primary focus of the House gradually shifted from education to service. It became less Presbyterian, more Salvation Army. The Community's annual

Daffodil Fair helped raise funds to keep the House going, as did the busy thrift shop, which provided used clothes for needy people.

The developing area of the Community's corporate work was on Iona itself. The restored Abbey attracted many visitors, including the Queen Mother. The Abbey season was extended to cater for the numbers interested, lasting from spring till late autumn. Courses on worship, healing, politics and peace attracted people from all over the world. Under the wardenship of John Harvey, who had been part of the Gorbals Group experiment, the Iona resident group itself became an all-year-round experiment in community. In a life of sharing of work and worship, the work and worth of each member of the group was valued, symbolized by the policy of equal pay. The Iona courses expressed the Community's central emphases; a total gospel which held together worship and work, prayer and politics, personal and corporate healing, peace and justice. The fact that these matters were discussed in the context of a worshipping, sharing community in a place of inspiration was crucial. Iona Abbey is not, and never has been, a conference centre.

The inspiration of what happens on Iona has been constant, amidst the ups and downs and struggles of the Iona Community's life. Through ministry on Iona, people's lives have been changed and the process continued right through the troubled 1970s. People who arrived at the jetty on Iona tired and depressed very often left a week later changed and invigorated, ready to face again the challenge of living a Christian witness in the situation from which they had come. Even the staff on Iona were hard put to describe what had happened. It could only be hinted at in language suggestive of the beating of wings — the Wild Goose at work through, and sometimes despite, the situation.

One of the saving things for the Iona Community was that even when it was tempted to spend all its energies on itself and its own concerns, it was not permitted to do so. People arriving on the shores of Iona from inner-city Glasgow, London, Europe, Asia or North America, seeking meaning, healing, challenge and a word of inspiration, would not let the Community be introspective or self-obsessed for long. Nor would they allow the Community to stay with too narrow a focus, such as peace. One temptation for the Community was to seek one simple 'line' and be a pressure group but the Iona pilgrims required more than single-issue agitation.

In the midst of troubled questioning and repeated doubt about the relevance of the Church, the youth work on Iona and at Camas (now developed considerably by an all-year resident community under the leadership of Deryck and Pat Collingwood) also provided encouragement and even light relief. The vitality and irreverent challenges brought by young people kept the Community on the move. The Iona youth work was now carried out in the old 'Rome Express' — the huts formerly used for the Abbey rebuilding. The presence of so many young people at worship in the Abbey church was a further test for the Community: the twice-daily services might be attended by Protestants, Roman Catholics, theologians, liturgical experts and young people from inner-city Glasgow who had never been inside a church building in their lives. The young people did not allow the Community to live on its memories. Many returned to work on the Abbey staff and some went on to become Associates or full members of Community.

Under Ian Reid's leadership, the Iona Community became more of a corporate body, with members taking fuller responsibility for the life of the Community. He built up an organization which was capable of sustaining the Community over the long haul. It was a measure of his personality that he was able to do this at a time when the glamour of being a member of the Community was less evident. He encouraged the gifts of the diverse membership, many of whom worked in difficult situations.

Leith Fisher was leader of a youth club in Calton, a run-down inner city area of Glasgow. He wrote in *The Coracle*:

> Calton is an eminently warm-hearted place, perhaps with a slight tendency to overheat. One of our most important functions is to affirm and articulate all that is positive already in the life of the place. In terms of the helping professionals who are in the community our place is fairly unique in that we have neither a statutory, educational or medical axe to grind, nor do we necessarily come into situations like most social workers, only after some sort of breakdown. This can be very important in the kind of relationships we can develop with people; simply human with no strings attached; and in the kind of role we can play in the community. It is surely central to the mission of the Church to affirm people's humanity.

Commenting on the experimental nature of the work, the Calton leader observed:

> There is tension between the old and the new throughout the whole enterprise. People think of our approach as 'experimental'. We are seen, and to some extent see ourselves, as doing something different. Many within the Church, it seems, await eagerly the day when we reach maturity and become 'real ministers'. We are certainly outwith the established structures of the Church, and we do feel pioneers in the sense that we are groping for a way into a situation which is not known and obvious . . . We stand in a tradition, but to make the tradition real we must dare to do new things. The purpose of the 'experiment' is to penetrate the life of a community. And this is not done in six months or even six years. Depending on where you stand, our work can look either curiously avant-garde or dangerously reactionary; perhaps the best place to be standing is somewhere in Calton itself.

The work of members ranged through race relations, education, social work, music and politics. Parish ministry in Scotland was still an important area of the Community's work. Fred Booth, minister at Raploch, a housing scheme in Stirling, wrote:

> The Christian community only scratches the surface of local problems but at least we are scratching. By being near to the delinquency, poverty and mismanagement of resources we are strategically placed with a clear job to do, and the willing are already being deeply involved. There is no doubt the Church generally must understand better, and enter more, the suffering of our neighbours . . . Raploch will be here for many years to come and the Christian community will be committed to serving, shaping and saving it to the best of its ability, and reminding itself that faith is about sharing, not the survival of the fittest.

In 1974, Graeme Brown was elected leader when Ian Reid came to the end of his term. A Church of Scotland missionary who had studied at Edinburgh, Cambridge and Heidelberg, he was ordained a minister of the Presbyterian Church of Nigeria. After the Nigerian civil war, he was appointed principal of St Columba's Theological College, South Africa. His activities in protest against apartheid meant that when he went home to Scotland at the end of his first tour of duty he was not permitted to return to his job. The continuing turmoil of questions within the Community, combined with shrinking resources, ensured that his time of leadership would not be easy. 'Experiment is not something that can be turned on like a tap', he wrote.

> New insights cannot be conjured up like rabbits from a hat. They arise, sometimes painfully, often out of much agonizing.

> The gropings of any group of Christians will always be tentative, their conclusions provisional. The only guideline to which members of the Community have consistently held over the years has been: 'Follow the light that you see, and pray for more light.' Significantly, that apothegm enshrines two quite clear convictions of the Iona Community — firstly, that there is light to be glimpsed; secondly, that it is on those at prayer that the light rises.

In war-torn Nigeria and troubled South Africa, Graeme Brown had seen the urgent need for a united Church. Under his leadership, the ecumenical dimensions of the Community's work were extended. Students from a Roman Catholic seminary in Scotland participated in theological student weeks on Iona and helped lead youth camps. In 1976, Chris Mercer, a social worker living in a community in Easterhouse, Glasgow, became the first Roman Catholic member of the Iona Community.

George MacLeod remained a loyal member, but his restiveness was still in evidence. He spent a great deal of time speaking and lobbying on the peace issue, at a time when arms agreements between the super powers had taken some of the steam out of the peace movement. He also kept up his campaign against the international financiers.

Fed up with what he saw as a capitulation to secularism, MacLeod flirted with the burgeoning charismatic movement. He was impressed by the Spirit-dependent theology of the Pentecostals, who made no concessions to the modern spirit. Their trumpet had no uncertain voice. He advocated charismatic themes within a largely unimpressed Iona Community. He also put his energy into a new movement, 'Mobilization for Survival', which sought signed-up supporters for a renewed campaign against the ever-growing arms race.

The Iona founder's disenchantment was also seen in another experiment he initiated, called 'The Fuinary Intention'. He established a small community at Fuinary with the aim of promoting a simple lifestyle and peace, but the experiment did not last long. Frustrated by his inability to persuade the Community to follow his more radical, global, single-minded concerns, MacLeod embraced his new causes with enthusiasm. 'What's George on about now?' was a common reaction within the Community at the time.

Graeme Brown continued the emphases of his predecessor, both in building up the corporate life of the Community and encouraging the gifts of its scattered membership. He saw his role as primarily an enabling one. From his background of work in Africa, he kept the concerns of the Third World on the Community's agenda. He and his family chose to live in the huge Glasgow housing scheme of Easterhouse, and he gave particular encouragement to those engaged in urban mission and service.

Members continued to break new ground. Ian Cowie moved from an inner-city team ministry to become full-time secretary of the Christian Fellowship of Healing. Working from central premises in Edinburgh, the Fellowship has ministered to many people. Explaining to fellow members the thinking behind the new centre, staffed by volunteers, Ian Cowie observed:

> We felt that what is needed today in the city is that we should be available to people when they need and when they can manage, instead of expecting them to come to meetings and services at times fixed by others.

The task of enabling the whole Church to be the people of God was a strong emphasis of the Iona Community at this time, and no one embodied this more at the parish level than Jack Orr, whose involvement of lay people in the housing scheme community of Oxgangs in Edinburgh is widely regarded as a model. Jack speaks for many Iona Community parish ministers as he recalls how the Community influenced his life and helped to shape his ministry:

Attending classes, in between playing football for Glasgow University, I chanced to read *We Shall Rebuild*, and it immediately struck a chord within me. Although my older brother, David, was youth secretary of the Iona Community, and although I had resumed my training for the ministry having been invalided out of the RAF, I knew little about either Iona or the Community. However, the chance to visit Iona Abbey for a students' week confirmed what I had felt about George's book, and I joined the Community when I became a minister. I spent the glorious summer of 1949 'rebuilding the abbey', or more precisely shovelling dirt out of the undercroft.

I then went for two years to the Old Kirk in West Pilton to work as assistant in a team ministry with Ian Reid. There I met and quickly (and wisely) married Janet. That was in the days when, attending Community Week, I had to live in the Abbey and Janet in the youth camp. It was to be some years before we were able to rent a house for a few weeks in Iona so that with our growing family of four we were able to spend our summer holidays there. By this time the Community had become a very central and important part both of my working and of my personal life. And so it has remained, both for myself and our family, two of whom are now very active Community members.

After six years in a thriving mining parish, I came to be first minister in Oxgangs, a new housing area in Edinburgh, where I have been ever since. In the solitary work of a minister, from the beginning I have found great friendship, help, support, encouragement and challenge from my membership of the Community. I suppose one should find these things in a Presbytery: but that, I am sure, is rarely the case. If, as I think, I have been a faithful and active member for nearly forty years, it has been because I have received so much from the Community and it has meant so much to me. I have also been enriched by having Community members working with me. At times I have been afraid that plenaries were becoming too much like Presbytery meetings (which has never been their purpose or their value), but that danger has been averted and is certainly not the case today.

Not only has the Iona Community meant a great deal to me, it has come to mean much to many people, young and old, Protestant and Roman Catholic, church member and non-member in Oxgangs, whom I have introduced to Iona Abbey and the Community. For it has always been a great pleasure to me that I have been able to take, or been responsible for, groups of all kinds going to stay in the Abbey or the youth camp, and the contacts and relationships built up between Oxgangs and Iona are very valuable and far-reaching.

A decisive year in the life of the Iona Community was 1977. Ralph Morton died, as did John Summers, a senior member who had given much of his life to South Africa. A further shock was news of the deterioration of the fabric of Community House. Costed options were looked at and the Community, desperately hard-pressed for finance, decided to move. It felt like the end of another era. A corporate sense of bereavement was in the air.

Latterly, the work of Community House had been symbolized by one of the services it offered — washing the feet of poor, tired, desperate and derelict people. The warden, Campbell Robertson, was known throughout Scotland as an authority on the problems of adult single homeless people. The departure from Clyde Street left a gap not just in the lives of Glasgow people, but in the heart of the Iona Community itself. Ralph Morton had written in an article which, sadly, he was unable to complete:

It's the end of a chapter, the loss of an old friend. And perhaps worse, it carries hints of failure and defeat. But in our sadness at the loss of a building, it's as well to remember that Community House was more than a building. It was a house where work was done and people met and in which some lived as their home. What made it distinctive was not its position or its architecture, but the life that went on in it.

And life is never the same; it is always changing. As we look back to the beginning and trace the changes that marked the thirty-three years of the House's history, we realize that we have never any right to say that the original pattern must be maintained unaltered or, if altered, it indicates declension.

Graeme Brown saw the move from Community House as an opportunity to do something different. He argued that the Community needed to learn to travel much more lightly and put its resources into people rather than plant. He advocated training by extension — a method of theological education pioneered in South America, by which people training for ministry continued in their secular employment, with church staff providing home study material and on-the-spot tutoring..

It was ironic that, despite seeking to travel light, the Community soon became bogged down in problems over property. After a move to one set of premises, another building was purchased for office accommodation. Problems with dry rot seemed to go on and on, taking up the time of staff and members and draining the Community's meagre resources.

The dry rot seemed to be a message. Here was a reforming movement exhibiting many of the signs of the Church it was seeking to reform — obsession with buildings, introspection, institutionalization. The question had to be asked: had the Community now served its purpose and was this the time to call it quits? Some members voted with their feet as the debates dragged on.

The Community was facing a midlife crisis. It had been in existence for more than forty years, long enough to develop a tradition worth defending. It was old enough to have become mellow. On the way, it had accumulated assumptions, buildings, staff, projects, sometimes in a rather confused and unclear way. Now, in the midst of an inflationary blizzard, it faced a crisis of identity.

In reviewing its history, its assets and its opportunities, the Community decided that it must continue. To quit now would be to abandon its responsibilities. A review of its organization produced a new plan of action. Three main areas were identified: Justice and

Peace, Work and the New Economic Order, and Community and Celebration.

Besides, there was still Iona itself. Or was there? The year 1979 saw the shock news that the Duke of Argyll was planning to sell the island in order to pay off death duties. There were rumours of purchase by oil-rich Arabs or the leisure industry. A public fund to purchase the island was established. The situation was saved by the Sir Hugh Fraser Foundation, which purchased the island for £1,500,000 and generously presented it to the nation in memory of Lord Fraser of Allander. The government asked the National Trust for Scotland to administer Iona and the public funds gathered were used to maintain the Abbey. The Iona Cathedral Trustees established a regular work squad with Attie MacKechnie, a member of the Iona Community resident in Mull, as its foreman.

The island was safe for posterity. The position of the Iona Community was less secure.

11

Learning to Fly Again

When Groucho Marx was asked what it felt like to be ninety years old, he replied that it was better than the alternative. The Iona Community, having decided that it too preferred life to the alternative, set about making a new beginning. Graeme Brown, who retired from the leadership at the end of his seven-year term in 1981, had led the Community through a dark period to the point at which it was able to make a fresh start.

I had been asked to stand for election to the leadership but had, for a number of reasons, declined. George MacLeod asked to see me in his room in the Abbey after the Hallowing Service at which new members of the Community were dedicated. It was after midnight. When I went into his room, he locked the door, opened his cupboard, then poured me the largest whisky I have ever seen, never mind attempted to consume. He sat down and spoke for ten minutes, laying out concisely his reasons for believing I should take on the job. Then he indicated that he did not wish me to respond, that it was late, that I should let him know my decision in a few days, and that he would respect that decision.

To be thus directly addressed in Iona Abbey after midnight by George MacLeod (then aged eighty-six), while three-quarters of the way through a tumblerful of whisky, is the nearest experience on earth to hearing the voice of the Holy Spirit that I can imagine! I knew in that instant, if I had not known before, the reason why so many people had joined George MacLeod in his ventures and been astonished to find themselves doing things of which they 'knew' they were incapable. I accepted.

A new start required a new home. The Glasgow base moved to the Pearce Institute in Govan, into the flat which had served as the manse of the minister of Govan Old Parish Church. The Pearce Institute was a huge community centre with a restaurant at its heart and a teeming life — the feel was not unlike that of the old Community House. In more ways than one, it felt like coming home.

At the same time, the Community, acting along with Christian Aid and the Balmore Trust, opened a justice and peace centre in Glasgow. Centrepeace sold Third World crafts and raised awareness of development issues. Helen Steven, the Iona Community's full-time justice and peace worker, found herself in demand to lead training sessions on non-violent action for peace. A Quaker and pacifist, Helen twice elected to go to prison rather than pay a fine for her part in peaceful anti-nuclear protests. The Community's peace and justice work increased, both in terms of training church members, and in organizing worship events at the sites of military installations.

The appointment of the Revds Ian and Kathy Galloway as joint Wardens of Iona Abbey heralded further developments on the island. Both ordained ministers of the Church of Scotland, the husband and wife team had lived in community in the Pilton housing scheme of Edinburgh. Their gifts in leading worship and in imaginative education attracted a new constituency to the old Abbey. Young adults came in increasing numbers. Theologians of conservative traditions (and some members of the Iona Community) now had to cope with the regular sight of a woman presiding at what had been a male preserve for centuries — the marble communion table of Iona Abbey. A biannual *Feisd* (Gaelic for festival) saw colourful tents and a marquee pitched in the grounds of the Abbey to cope with the number of youngsters from different parts of the world.

The marquee and tents were also required for the annual summer gathering of members of the Community. Spouses and children were welcome at what was now a family festival as well as a members' conference. Indeed, the Community was becoming much more of an extended family. A commission was established to see what changes were required as a result of a rapid growth in membership.

Why such an upsurge in interest? There are times and seasons in the development of communities and it is often difficult to pinpoint the reasons. Part of it was due to a wider change of mood. The idealism and questioning of the 1960s and 70s had given way to scepticism and a search for answers. Experimenting communities such as Taizé, Corrymeela and Iona allowed people to test out their Christian faith without making binding institutional commitments. The ecumenical dimension of their life appealed to young people in particular, as did the emphasis on work for justice and peace as an expression of Christian faith. The escalating arms race, in spite of previous arms limitation agreements, demanded a response from Christians, and radical ecumenical communities were able to be much less equivocal than the churches.

A further factor in the renewal of interest was the growing awareness that Christianity is a community-based faith. The individual is called to be a disciple in the context of a supporting and demanding community. The lack of community evident in much church life compelled people to look elsewhere for Christian support and challenge.

The influx of new young members from different denominations and with varying degrees of formal church allegiance posed the question as to whether the Iona Community was a movement within the Church or an alternative to the Church. It was a problem which Ian Reid had identified but which had not been resolved. Some of the members were deeply involved in the life of the institutional Church while others were not. The Community's response was to ride both horses in the ring and say that somebody had to try — the nature of the Kingdom of God was such that no single approach would do.

The life of the Iona Community could never be described simply in terms of its corporate work on island or mainland — the variety of activities engaged in by members and Associates constitutes its most important outreach. Some members are unemployed — like Chris Mercer, a Roman Catholic social worker who is disabled and has used the time at her disposal to campaign on behalf of disabled people and the tenants in the high flats in Glasgow in which she lives. A few examples will give a feel for the range of membership in the 1980s.

Robin Ross, while Church of Scotland minister in Tiberias on the Sea of Galilee, in charge of a centre which used to be a mission hospital to promote the conversion of the Jews but is now used as a place of hospitality, reflected on how the model of Iona has been a constant influence over the past few years — with hospitality as a keynote:

> Hospitality to pilgrims — reminding them that the value of pilgrimage is proved in going home again. Echoing the hurt of the local church, mainly Arabic-speaking, who watch pilgrims troop through their places of worship like museums and who do not seem to see the worshippers. God chose humans to be His holy places, yet the Arab Christians are still so isolated and ignored.

> Hospitality to our neighbours — Jews, Moslems, Christians, Druze, Israelis, Palestinians and so on — such alien confusion. And all the time the temptation to interpret mission as the means whereby we force others to conform to our mould so that we will feel comfortable with them.

> In Israel you still smell the gas and the smoke of the death camps — you can't avoid the bitterness of the displaced Palestinians — so often you wonder where you can unobtrusively dump this rather problematic package called the Gospel of reconciliation.

> This is a loony place — but the Iona Community's a loony community, and so there is a sense that folk understand some of the confusion, frustration, excitement, wonder — for in the isolation there is still a lifeline of accountability to real people.

Raymond Young who later held a senior post within Scottish Homes, was Director (Scotland) of the Housing Corporation, a Government-sponsored agency set up to promote, register, supervise and fund non-profitmaking housing associations. Part of his work consisted of supporting people in inner-city areas and housing estates — which he saws as a means of empowering people. He said:

> Housing is only part of the multiple deprivation of such areas. These are societies characterized by

dependency and hopelessness, with a continuing downward spiral. I sometimes say that the difference between the rich areas and the poor areas is that the people in the wealthy areas know how to manipulate the system to their own and others' advantage. So while we market housing associations as a way of improving housing conditions, we are providing people with training in collective power, and helping to unlock latent abilities. While I have to care for all the different types of associations, the work which really inspires me is empowering groups of local residents. It's a long-term process — we will not see the full benefits for two or three generations. In some ways it's a bit like decolonialization — Govan and Malawi have things in common!

How does my membership of the Iona Community affect all this? Firstly, it got me into it. I came to Govan in 1969 as a student, with some ideas about providing a technical service to enable inner-city residents to improve their own housing. I came under the influence of David Orr, and realized that the empowering view of the Gospel which I generally held had been inspired by George MacLeod. Iona, which I first visited in 1970, seemed like home. And the Community has remained home — even when I pulled out. And I had to come back in — this time as a family.

Secondly, the Community is not just another club. It's a base for the whole family, and most of my closest friends are in it. It has a pervasive effect on my life. I don't wear my membership on my sleeve at work, but I'm sure it affects how I relate to those working with me and my judgement when making decisions.

Thirdly, the Iona Community has kept me in the Church (of which I regularly despair) and challenges me, when regularly tempted, back to the empowering power of the Gospel. It certainly does not make life

comfortable, but it helps to make life bearable —
there are enough other 'nutters' to share the tension.

Pat Welburn, while Principal Officer (child care) for a Catholic
Diocesan Child Care agency based in York, was involved in recruiting,
training and approving families to adopt children of all ages, and
supporting and counselling pregnant girls; she also provided court
reports in care proceedings. Reflecting on her work, she observed:

> Supervising the professional work of a small agency
> and working independently for the court can be
> professionally lonely, and I am often faced with having
> to make difficult decisions with little support. My
> membership of the Iona Community helps me fit
> my work into the context of much wider issues of
> which I am constantly being made aware. Although
> I cannot share details of my work because of
> confidentiality, I can get support from members on
> principles. I also find the Community's view of
> Christianity being a bridge rather than a doormat a
> great support when I have to make recommendations
> to protect a child — recommendations which I know
> are going to hurt some adults.
>
> Although my Catholic faith is important to me, my
> membership of the Iona Community unites me with
> other Christians with different shades of belief, and
> that's important too.

Stuart MacQuarrie now a local government councillor was in the
1980s a Church of Scotland minister in Toryglen housing scheme,
Glasgow, where much of his work lay in breaking down prejudice
between Protestants and Roman Catholics. He related:

> An irate parent demanded an interview with the head
> teacher of a large secondary school in Glasgow. 'My
> children are being indoctrinated by your religious
> education teacher', he claimed. 'They're hearing
> about Roman Catholics!' The head teacher patiently
> explained that in the religious education classes the
> pupils would learn about all the great faiths and
> religions of the world. It was education, not

indoctrination. The parent refuse to budge. 'I don't want my children to hear anything about Roman Catholics', he shouted. In exasperation, the head teacher said that the pupils learned how to cook and bake, but that didn't make them into cakes: in science they learned about nuclear fission, but that didn't make them radioactive. 'Oh!' replied the parent, 'fishin's OK. I do a bit of that myself from time to time!'

That incident actually happened. Not in the dim and distant past, but in 1987. In a way it illustrates the confusions of the Christian faith in this part of the world. All the subversive forces of prejudice, ignorance and bigotry work with each other, pervading lives. Even our other national religion, football, recognizes and strengthens the prejudices — Celtic, the Roman Catholic team with strong links to the south of Ireland, and Rangers, standing for Unionist Britain and Protestantism. Only recently have Rangers played a Roman Catholic in their team — not because of anything the churches or the Iona Community have said or done, but for purely capitalist reasons.

How do the churches cope with this at a parish level? In Toryglen there are two churches, one Protestant and the other Roman Catholic. The people of these churches all through the week go to the same shops together, go on buses to the city centre together, and go to the pubs together. On Sundays they go to separate churches. In 1985, for the first time ever, both churches did something together. We went to Iona, for a weekend of sharing and learning. From that weekend, we have worshipped together in each others' churches. We have shared together socially — small steps, moving together in pilgrimage. For me, this would not have been possible had I not received the support and encouragement of the Iona Community, who showed me that Christian faith is not a retreat into armed camps, but a journey.

And in this place of confusions where faith and allegiance to football clubs go hand in hand, there is always hope. A lady in my church told me of how she had been to Rome with her next door neighbour to see the Pope. 'He waved to us,' she said. 'And what's more, the money which paid for the trip was won by my husband on the Rangers pools! '

Lastly, Peter Millar, then a minister of the Church of South India in Madras and now warden on Iona, reported:

What does the Iona Community mean to a member living six thousand miles away from Scotland? The short answer — a lot. Such 'meaning' may refuse an easy definition, but it is real, none the less. Perhaps mentioning a concrete situation would underline the feeling of solidarity, of shared perception, which in a global context is one of the strengths of the Community.

Part of our work here in South India involves sharing with desperately poor families living in village areas. Now that summer has come, many of these families have little or no water. One day I was in one such village, about sixty miles from Madras, and the local people were telling me about their struggles. No water, no work in the fields, no fodder for the cattle and hardly enough rice left over for one decent meal a day. And although you discover in such circumstances the great inner resources of village families, you also feel helpless and angry at the injustice of it all. How can they bear it, year after year? Will things ever change for the poor?

Then I remember, sitting in that poor village under a burning sun, that I am part of a group of people who are equally concerned. And together we are a people of prayer for whom worship and the search for justice and peace are connected. And it's exactly at that point that the Iona Community becomes a flesh and blood thing. We are on a journey together — whether in

Madras or Glasgow or Lusaka or Pilton. And despite
our differences, we are trying to listen to one another
and to God.

Shared prayer: shared concerns: shared hopes and a
shared appreciation of one another, and also, along
the way, many failures. We are a Community of hope
— and life, even when it's 103 degrees in the shade
and all you want is a glass of water!

Ministers, chaplains, teachers, miners, social workers, doctors,
housewives, civil engineers, politicians, unemployed, community
work volunteers, craft co-operative workers, industrial managers,
youth and community workers, librarian, herdsman, small-holder,
clerk of works, musician, artist, race relations worker, hospital ward
housekeeper, newspaperman, drugs specialist, YMCA secretary, Third
World shop manager, legal assistant, psychotherapist, VSO organizer,
students' union president: these represent some of the facets of the
180-plus membership of the Iona Community in the 1980s. The
850 Associates and 2500 Friends of the Community represent an
even wider range of activity and interest. (The current figures are
215 Members, 1400 Associates and 1600 Friends.)

One of the issues which demanded a response from the Iona
Community in the 1980s was unemployment. The Community,
which had been born out of a situation of high unemployment,
proposed to the General Assembly of the Church of Scotland that a
special ministry be created, enabling the resources of the Church to
be mobilized. The Assembly turned down the proposal by a narrow
majority. The Community was determined that such an appointment
should be made, and it decided to sell its collection of valuable
paintings to make it possible. The Revd Walter Fyfe, who was
appointed, felt that responses based on charity were inadequate. A
former member of the Gorbals Group, he was convinced that
unemployed and poorly-paid people in deprived areas needed more
power over the direction of their own lives. He helped train groups
to establish credit unions, enabling people to invest or borrow money
without getting into the hands of the loan sharks. He also helped
communities to establish food co-operatives — another form of local
power which gave people confidence to tackle wider issues.
Commenting on the difficulty of moving towards a new view of
work, Walter Fyfe observes:

The debate on unemployment and poverty both within and outside the churches has taken place on a very narrow 'authorized' political platform. Conservatives, as they have done for the whole of history, artificially create unemployment and poverty to benefit the rich and powerful: the Labour Party, as they have done since their inception, have harked back to dogmas such as 'full employment', 'increased social benefits', 'public works' and so on. But any worker in any private or nationalized industry in the so-called era of 'full employment' (when seventy per cent of school leavers in Gorbals were without work for two years at least) will speak of degrading, mindless, dangerous or unhealthy or just plain boring and meaningless jobs. They want to get away from all that, yet their political party want to return them to old days and old employers. It is as if Moses had negotiated with Pharaoh for extra supplies of straw to normalize the brick-building industry of Egypt.

With the growth of new technology, it was clear that fewer people would have paid work and those out of work would suffer badly. A new way had to be found to share work and wealth — the Christian Church could not stand back and do nothing. New models of economic justice had to be developed. The Iona Community's insistence that new ideas had to be incarnated rather than simply expressed on paper resulted in three modest attempts at worksharing: Ian and Kathy Galloway on Iona; Duncan and Marlene Finlayson, in charge of the Abbey shop; and John Bell and Graham Maule, joint youth co-ordinators.

John Bell and Graham Maule, in their new joint appointment, initiated an imaginative youth volunteer scheme. Young people who were on the dole often felt themselves devalued, with no role to play in the life of the Church. Programmes were devised to enable young people to live together in Christian community in deprived areas and make themselves available for service. They were given 'hard to let' accommodation in council housing schemes and, as they 'signed on' at the local dole office, they befriended other youngsters in similar situations. Drug and other problems were addressed, and in the process the youth volunteers themselves learned a great deal about their own talents and limitations. They met for training and, both on Iona and the mainland, came together to reflect on their experiences. Unemployed young people who went to Iona and were moved by what they experienced could be offered a place on the youth volunteer scheme rather than simply drift back into what they felt was a purposeless existence.

The houses where the young people lived together were known as 'Columban Houses'. These were a low-key experiment launched by the Iona Community in 1982, designed to explore new models of Christian community appropriate to urban situations. Columban Houses were small communities with the declared aim of incarnating the concerns of the Iona Community. Some were council house communities in deprived areas, such as those lived in by the youth volunteers. Others were shared living arrangements involving two or more houses in a neighbourhood. Others again were extended family situations with an emphasis on Christian lifestyle. Several houses were quickly established in Scotland, another in a multi-racial area in Birmingham, two in the London area, one in the USA and one in India.

A radical training experiment which linked together the Community's resources on Iona and the mainland took shape in the 'Peregrini' project. As we have seen, historically the Peregrini were Columba's Celtic wandering barefoot preachers, who walked the highways and byways sharing the gospel story. They were trained in community on Iona, then travelled light as they made their way. Would it be possible to wed the Celtic notion of the Peregrini to today's situation, and produce a training scheme which would take seriously the gifts and talents of unemployed people?

Lynn Brady and Lizz Spence, two former Iona youth volunteers who had lived in Columban House communities, volunteered to be guinea pigs for the experiment, and an experience-based training scheme was drawn up in consultation with them. They worked in parish and community situations in Edinburgh and reflected on what they were doing in the light of the biblical message. After eight months on the mainland, they went to Iona for further training in leading worship, theological reflection and life in community. At the end of the year's programme, Lizz went to work at a Church of Scotland arts centre and Lynn was appointed to a church post in Pakistan.

The experience convinced the Iona Community of the need for new methods of lay training, which took account of the gifts and experience of the Church's membership at every level. It also confirmed the tremendous potential of the Community's resources on Iona and the mainland for such new ventures.

The 1980s have seen a renewed interest in the worship of the Iona Community. This was in part due to the leadership of worship at the Abbey, where the historical and ecumenical dimensions of Iona were wed to contemporary concerns to a way which was seen to be relevant and appropriate. The development of new music and drama on Iona interested the Church at large, as ways were sought to breathe new life into Sunday mornings.

The remarkable gifts of John Bell and Graham Maule also brought new flair to the Community's worship. John Bell's ability to write poetic words which express Christian themes in contemporary terms, and to compose music which is both imaginative and singable, has made him one of the Church's outstanding leaders of worship. He and Graham Maule also produced drama scripts for worship, and Graham's abilities as an artist were used to provide illustrations for the new materials. The two established the Wild Goose Worship Group, composed of young people who go to churches and conferences to work with people on new ways of worship. John and Graham paraphrased the early verses of John's Gospel as follows:

> Before the world began
> One word was there;
> Grounded in God he was,
> Rooted in care;
> By him all things were made,
> In him was love displayed,
> Through him God spoke and said,
> 'I am for you'.
>
> Life found in him its source,
> Death found its end;
> Light found in him its course,
> Darkness its friend;
> For neither death nor doubt
> Nor darkness can put out
> The glow of God, the shout:
> 'I am for you'.

The Word was in the world
Which from him came;
Unrecognized he was,
Unknown by name;
One with all humankind,
With the unloved aligned,
Convincing sight and mind:
'I am for you'.

All who received the Word
By God were blessed;
Sisters and brothers they
Of earth's fond guest.
So did the Word of Grace
Proclaim in time and space,
And with a human face,
'I am for you'.

The worship materials were published by a newly established division of the Iona Community's work — Wild Goose Publications. The Community's former publications wing, built up over many years by John Morison and Mary MacKechnie, had not been in operation for some time. Song collections such as *Songs of the Incarnation* met a demand within the churches, as did three new volumes of Wild Goose Songs. Sales of records and cassettes of the new Iona worship — *Through Wood and Nails*, *The Touching Place*, *Folly and Love*, *Cloth for the Cradle* — showed the hunger for new and lively worship forms. John Bell and Graham Maule visited churches in the USA where the new material found a welcome response. Wild Goose Publications also published pamphlets on the concerns of the Iona Community, and a collection of George MacLeod's prayers, *The Whole Earth Shall Cry Glory*.

When Pope John Paul II came to Scotland in 1982 and issued his call to Scottish Christians to go on pilgrimage together 'hand in hand', the Iona Community responded by inviting the leaders of all the Scottish Churches to come to Iona to worship and study the Bible together. The Scottish Church Leaders' Gathering at Iona at Pentecost 1984 was a historic assembly. The Moderator of the General Assembly of the Church of Scotland and the Roman Catholic Archbishop of Glasgow were among the leaders of the main Scottish denominations present. The shared worship and Bible study was an important piece of symbolism in a Scotland still badly affected by religious division. The church dignitaries not only shared study and meeting. Like all other guests at the Abbey, they participated in chores — the washing of dishes and the preparation and serving of meals. In the context of Christian community, all the participants pledged themselves to work for the unity of the Church. At the Healing service in Iona Abbey, the Most Revd Thomas Winning, now Cardinal Winning but then Roman Catholic Archbishop of Glasgow, declared:

> The path to further reconciliation to my mind cannot lie in brooding over our wounds, or in mutual recriminations, but in a continual series of creative experiments born of goodwill and with a vision of the future which we are building together. The churches have therefore above all to be open to the unifying power of the Spirit. If we are static, immobile, motionless, there will be no room for the Spirit. If the Church is static, it will not command the response from the Lord to come to its aid. But against a Church on the move, open to the Spirit, the gates of hell will never prevail.

Iona, home to Protestant and Roman Catholic alike, has become increasingly a centre of ecumenical pilgrimage. A joint group from Ireland headed by Cardinal Tomas O' Fiach and the Revd Dr Ray Davey, Presbyterian founder of the Corrymeela Community, went on pilgrimage to Iona and worshipped together in the Abbey. The Anglican Bishop of Liverpool, David Sheppard, and the Roman Catholic Archbishop of Liverpool, Derek Worlock, led an ecumenical pilgrimage of young people. They studied the work of the youth volunteers in Glasgow, staying at Columban Houses, before going on to Iona to spend a week together at the youth camp. Joint Protestant-Catholic parish groups used Iona as a place to reflect on what was happening back home.

When it became clear that the old huts which served as the youth camp were nearing the end of their useful life, the Iona Community was faced with a critical decision. Should it repair the old huts once again? Should it build a new centre? Or should youth work be discontinued on the island? The Community, recognizing that many, many young people had experienced life-changing events on Iona, agreed that the work must continue. After looking at all the options, the Community decided for a purpose-built centre which would also accommodate families and provide facilities for disabled people.

It was decided to call the new building the MacLeod Centre, in honour of the Community's founder. George MacLeod himself, having moved away from some of his former concerns, had come to a new appreciation of the Community, as the Community had of its founder. He had learned to let go, and the Community had learned the difficult art of Living Without Father while father was still around. The celebration of George MacLeod's ninetieth birthday in Govan in 1985 was a very happy and renewing event in the life of the Community.

The design for the MacLeod Centre was chosen as a result of an international architectural competition which attracted 191 entries. The winners, Feilden Clegg Design of Bath, produced a design which combined traditional island features with an innovative use of internal space. The style of building was welcomed on the island, where relationships with the Community have been much warmer in recent years.

The Community then set about the daunting task of raising the £900,000 needed to build the new Centre. The 'Go 90' appeal invited people to give ninety hours' work or raise £90 - £1 for every year of George MacLeod's life. Maxwell MacLeod, eldest son of Lord and the late Lady MacLeod, was appointed joint appeal director, along with Alison Macdonald, former administrator at Iona Abbey.

George MacLeod went to the USA in 1986 to promote the Centre and speak about the work of the Iona Community. At a convocation of American churches he became, at ninety-one, the ninth holder of the distinguished Union Medal. He had been a postgraduate student at Union Theological Seminary, New York, in 1924 and was visiting Harry Emerson Fosdick Professor in 1952. In his citation, President Donald W. Shriver said:

> What great cause of Church and society in our time has been untouched by your energy, eloquence, compassion, anger and disputatiousness? Who else has more abundantly demonstrated that social justice, church unity, and peace among the nations root together in the Gospel of Jesus Christ?

Yours has been the distinction of seeing connections well in advance of others. You connected us to our past. You founded the Iona Community and rebuilt Iona Abbey, because you knew your debt as a Scots Christian to the missionary passion of a sixth-century Celtic monk.

You connected that historic island to the mainland crisis of modern industrial Scotland. Thus you called the Church of your country to the dialectic of withdrawal from the world and return to its crying need. You connected the scattered fragments of Christ's Church to the call of their Lord in unity. You refused to settle down into ironic Reformation complacency. Having rebuilt the Abbey that your zealous Scots ancestors let fall into ruins, you reminded their descendants that the reform of reformation is perpetual for those subject to the restless Holy Spirit.

You have been called a 'lost cause' man, but we call you an advocate of ideas whose times have not yet come. How would they ever come without leadership like yours which is willing to be a minority for now in service of a majority to come?

The campaign to build the MacLeod Centre revealed the extent to which Iona and the work of the Community had touched the heart of countless lives. The money came steadily as a response of gratitude and as a commitment towards the future. The determination of so many people in different parts of the world to see that a new home for young people was built on Iona moved the Community. With a good part of the money raised in eighteen months, work began on site on Easter Monday, 1987. The foundation stone was laid on Columba's Day, 9 June 1987, by Lord MacLeod, assisted by Professor Vincent Harding — historian of the black struggle for justice in the USA and close associate of the late Revd Martin Luther King — and two young people, one Protestant and the other Roman Catholic.

The commitment to build the MacLeod Centre was a symbol of the Iona Community's determination to see Iona continue as a base for Christian community, unity, reconciliation and mission into the next millennium. The vision was that Iona once known as 'the University of the North', should be a campus for vocational learning in a troubled world. The honking of the Wild Goose would continue to be heard in the neighbourhood.

Part Three

ON A WING
AND A PRAYER

12

Communities of Resistance

Geese in a flock have seventy per cent greater range than a single goose on its own; geese in formation fly seventy-five per cent faster than single geese.

Iona, down through the centuries, speaks to us above all about the experience of the Holy Spirit in *community*. The islanders who have always had to be dependent on each other, the Celtic monks, the Benedictines and the present-day Iona Community have all learned about the need and strength of sharing.

Christianity is a community faith. The scriptures of the Old and New Testaments are products of a faith community and can only be understood as such. When Jesus began his ministry, he immediately gathered disciples round him. Right from the beginning, conversion meant a call to discipleship within the context of a community of faith. The New Testament is full of the struggles of the early Christian community as it sought to live out the faith which bound it together.

A key New Testament concept is represented by the Greek word *koinonia*, meaning communion or fellowship. Communion, community, communicate — these words of shared derivation speak of a shared experience and are at the heart of the Christian message. The church is intended to be such a community of participation, yet the actual experience of being in church is often one of isolation. The popularity of places such as Taizé, Corrymeela and Iona testifies to the hunger for community.

When guests come to live in Iona Abbey today, they come to share in the daily life of a resident community which worships and works together year in, year out. The Celtic and Benedictine insistence that all of life is sacred is reflected in the life of the contemporary Iona Community. The group resident in the Abbey all the year round tries to work out ways of living together in which resources are shared, people are valued and listened to, and love and trust can be evidenced, despite differences.

Sitting around a refectory table in any one week may be a professor of theology, a Roman Catholic monk, an unemployed teenager, a Quaker peace activist, an army chaplain, a single parent with children, a businessman, a battered wife, an inner-city gang boy and a Presbyterian minister. Many guests have had that experience common to all too many people in today's world — that of being buffeted, rejected and hurt so that they become closed and defensive. The Abbey community aims to be a group where people can feel safe — a sanctuary where they can open out, share their fears, reflect on their lives, share worship and work, and join in discussions on the theme for the week, in which contemporary issues are looked at in the light of the Gospel.

Community life — the life of the people who form each particular week's Abbey community — grows fast as people wash dishes together, worship, engage in arts or music, and chat — at the dinner table, in the common room or chapter house, on walks and out on the weekly pilgrimage round the island. During the course of the week people can expect to be affirmed — and challenged. The mix of age, colour, gender, background and religious affiliation expresses each week an amazing diversity of Christian community.

It would be easy — and wrong — to romanticize Christian community, especially in a location such as Iona. The tensions of living together are not magically dispersed; indeed, they may be increased because of the heightened expectations. The testimony of so many on Iona is that healing comes through living the questions and not accepting easy answers. Somehow, the Church at large must work at ways of restoring real community to its heart, and intentional communities such as Iona can offer hard-won experience in the quest for such an essential recovery. People are not attracted to communities such as Iona simply because of a need for community. It is a particular style of community which is important.

What is the style of the contemporary Iona community? Perhaps it can best be described by the word 'incarnational'.

The basis of a genuinely Christian radicalism is to be found in the opening verses of John's Gospel, 'The Word became flesh and dwelt among us'. The notion that the creator of the universe expressed himself not in ideas or words or telegrams but in a human being in a particular time and place, has always been a scandal and a stumbling block, but it is central to the Christian message. The Gospel is about the embodiment of the spiritual — the fleshing out of the eternal. Incarnation is God's mode, and his human style is that of a servant with a towel and a basin. No wonder Christianity can be so offensive to religious people!

The incarnational message of the Son of God is seen right at the start of his ministry, when he presented the words of Isaiah as his manifesto:

> The Spirit of the Lord is upon me, because he has anointed me to preach good news to the poor. He has sent me to proclaim release to the captives and recovering of sight to the blind, to set at liberty those who are oppressed, to proclaim the acceptable year of the Lord. (RSV: Isaiah 61:1-2; Luke 4: 18-19)

When John the Baptist's followers ask Jesus whether he is the Messiah, the reply is given:

> Go and tell John what you have seen and heard: the blind receive their sight, the lame walk, lepers are cleansed and the deaf hear, the dead are raised up, the poor have good news preached to them. And blessed is he who takes no offence at me. (RSV: Luke 7: 22)

The kingdom of God, then, is identifiable not by talk but by happenings. It is an embodied kingdom. Theology is not arid intellectual discussion of ideas, but reflection on the specifics of the inbreaking kingdom.

There have been times when the Iona Community confused the kingdom with talk and resolutions (and it has been at its grisly worst when it has tried to lecture everyone or talked as if it was going to Save the World), but on the whole it has tried and still tries to test its insights in here-and-now specifics. The Peregrini scheme, for example, was one in a line of experiments on behalf of the whole Church. The Community's maverick, non-establishment role gives it a flexibility and freedom to experiment that the institutional Church seems to lack (or chooses not to exercise). The Community does not regard failure as a terminal illness.

The Iona Community began with the here-and-now specifics of Govan in the Hungry Thirties. One of its continuing tasks is to draw the attention of the Church to its problematical task of urban mission. A Church which proclaims 'Good News to the poor' as a central platform cannot rest content with its position as a largely middle-class organization.

When I first joined the Iona Community in 1970, I went to minister in Easterhouse, a sprawling housing scheme on the outskirts of Glasgow. These Scottish Sowetos, tribal homelands of the disposable poor, are a problem for a kirk which is locked into a professional value system. In Easterhouse, less than one per cent of the population regularly attended any Protestant church. Large parts of Scotland — and England, according to the *Faith in the City* report — are alienated from the Church. They see the Church not as a fellowship of liberated and accepting people, but as a group of well-heeled, judgemental people who have been fortunate enough to have got their lives together. They see Christians as people who are comfortable with the military and the judiciary and the well-to-do, who will not do anything which will radically affect their own self-interest.

Why is this? One senior churchman put the blame firmly on the inhabitants of the housing schemes and inner-city areas, saying that the deprived areas should be renamed the 'depraved' areas. An easy answer: the people in the housing schemes and inner-city areas are more evil! It is as simple as that.

What a travesty of the great evangelical tradition that is! Protestantism is at its best when it is radical, freewheeling, inconoclastic, prophetic, refusing to bend the knee. When it degenerates into a prudential buttress for the powers-that-be, it sells Jesus down the river. And the people know it. They, as well as anyone, can sniff death in the air. (It is just as insulting and dehumanizing to romanticize the poor and present the oppressed as innocent refugees from Eden, as many guilt-ridden middle-class radicals do. Experience and theology cry out against it.) But many people sense death, not life, in the Church, which is seen as condemning the culture and values of ordinary people.

The tragedy is that the gospel of freedom in Jesus Christ comes over as a moralistic preference for professional values and an attack on working-class culture. Prudence and inoffensiveness seem much more highly valued than impetuous generosity and risk-taking.

The issue was focused for me while in India to visit Community member Peter Millar in Madras. To a large extent the Indian Church was shaped by Western missionaries who brought a vital faith, but also Western ways. The Indian Church learned Victorian songs, Victorian language, Victorian denominations. A Church dependent on foreign money was created. Christ called people to be different and in India to be Western was to be different. Many of the missionaries urged people to turn their backs on their own cultural heritage. They exchanged dhotis (simple cloth garments) for suits, Sanskrit chants for English songs, and enjoyed the benefits of foreign patronage. A major struggle within the Indian Church today is that of learning to be Indian and Christian without being Western, and to do so without feelings of inferiority.

The small and vulnerable churches in the housing schemes and inner-city areas have a similar struggle to form indigenous expressions of the faith over against a paternalistic, dominant Church and they do this at a time when the dominant Church itself is under enormous pressure and in a period of accelerating decline. The confident notion of the Church which George MacLeod articulated in the 1930s has collapsed. The Emperor's threadbare ecclesiastical clothes are in the Oxfam shop.

Attempts to take urban mission seriously over the past hundred years or so are well documented by John Harvey, then minister of Govan Old Parish Church, later, 1988-1995, Leader of the Community in his book, *Bridging the Gap: Has the Church Failed the Poor?* (Saint Andrew Press, 1987). The Iona Community has certainly not solved the 'problem' (indeed, setting the matter into a problem/ solution framework has itself been part of the problem). Its merit is that it has always recognized that there was a serious issue to be addressed and has trained people who then put their bodies where their theological mouths were. The strategy of training ordained men and women who would then make the system 'work' was a coherent and logical one, but the collapse of confidence in the traditional model of the Church has exposed its limitations. Columban Houses, the Youth Volunteer Scheme and the Peregrini project were modest, contemporary attempts to find new light and to follow it. New explorations both within and outside official church structures will be part of the Iona Community's continued commitment to the urban situation.

If an incarnational style is to be lived out in the urban, or any other, scene, it cannot be done alone. A Christian life which is both personal and corporate needs supportive community. If the Church as it stands does not provide that kind of supportive and accountable community, it must be created. Freedom and discipline are not alternatives: they are mutual parts of the Christian enterprise.

Dietrich Bonhoeffer talks about the need for 'holy worldly' people — followers of Jesus who live in the world but who are sustained by an arcane, or secret, discipline of prayer. 'Contemplation' or 'action' are false alternatives. Both are involved in a Christian lifestyle. A person who prays deeply will be driven to act against injustice. Similarly, a Christian who is engaged in the problems of the world will be driven to prayer. Contemplation need not be escapism, a turning one's back on the world which God loves. Prayer is at the heart of a genuine Christian radicalism — one which truly gets to the root of the matter.

It is matter which is at the root of the spiritual, if the Incarnation is to have its central place in our thinking. Our spirituality is tested in how we handle the material. But does that mean politics?

The issue was clarified for me on the Howrah Bridge, Calcutta. A young man was running through the traffic, pulling a rickshaw in which two adults were seated. The sweat poured down his face and his bare feet slapped out a rhythm on the hot, dusty road. He was a beast of burden; our host said he would die at a young age. Elsewhere in Calcutta, poor people died on the pavements.

Many, many people in the world have no home, little food, no money, few clothes, no bed. They die of disease or malnutrition at an early age. The rickshaw wallah pounding the streets of Calcutta, pulling fellow human beings for a few rupees, must make God cry. Of course you 'know' this intellectually; but that is different from seeing, feeling, smelling, touching. And when you look into the eyes of the poor, you become aware of your own complicity.

What to do? Living paralysed by guilt is no great help to the poor.

Love demands nothing less than a re-ordering of the world's priorities: a new economic and political order. I can only glimpse what that might mean: part of me is afraid to look any further at the implications. Justice is at the very heart of the faith, not an optional extra. And God's justice in the present situation is transformed into a word of prophetic judgement, whether we like it or not.

Charity is not enough. The work of Mother Teresa in caring for the dying is beautiful — but if nothing is done to change the overall arrangements of a world dominated by the 'Christian' West, the poor will die in the gutters of the Calcuttas of the world for all time.

Prayer is not about turning one's back on all this. Thomas Merton, a Roman Catholic monk who went into a monastery to escape the world, found himself in the silence addressed by a God who cares about the oppressed. Reflecting on Christian collusion with structures of injustice, Merton pointed out that the Pharisees knew how to arrange things in such a way that the poor would always be with them. We are challenged today to a deeper prayer and a tougher political analysis. If prayer is divorced from the hard-nosed politics of Christian love, it becomes self-indulgent, navel-gazing deep breathing. It will be an abomination to a free God who shouts 'Take this away from Me!' Politics on its own is not enough, either. If it is uprooted from the forgiving justice at the heart of God, it becomes hard, vengeful, unreformed and ultimately tyrannical.

Justice cannot be separated from peace, any more than prayer can be separated from action. The cost of fuelling the arms race is one million dollars each minute of the day — and while this is going on millions of people die of malnutrition. The price tag of this kind of 'peace' is too high and it is being paid in the blood of the poor.

'To me,' wrote a twenty-year-old officer in the trenches of Salonika in 1916,

> 'it does not matter one bit the fact that all these brave fellows were lost at Gallipoli and now we have retired; after all, when they died they were doing their utmost for the cause — and there, as far as the individual is concerned, the matter ends. Whether or no this particular charge was a success or failure; whether or no that or this general made a mistake; whether or no a whole expedition is a failure; that man has been

ordered to do a thing and has proceeded to do it,
and so far as he is concerned his job is done and well
done.'

The young officer, who went on to attack what he called 'mouse-eyed conscientious objectors', distinguished himself by winning the Military Cross and the Croix de Guerre in that 'war to end all wars'. His name was George Fielden MacLeod.

Somewhere along the line, the word 'No' has to be uttered in the name of a greater 'Yes'. We are called to be peace-makers, and that is a tough business. It is certainly not about being peace lovers (isn't everybody?) or about being passive-ists. The biblical word for peace — shalom — is a rich concept, involving right relationships with God and human beings. It is a tough, disciplined notion, not to be dispersed in the sentimental twanging of guitars. It is peace-with-justice, and it is cross-shaped.

To say 'No' in today's world in the name of a greater 'Yes' is hard to do alone. It requires communities of resistance, with prayer at their heart. Even silence. And the old Celtic idea of the anamchara, the soul friend, is ripe for revival.

At an isolated place on the island of Iona there is a circle of stones. It is called the Hermit's Cell. It testifies to the need for times of withdrawal, in order to go back to the demanding and joyful task of Christian community, a community which is not an end in itself but is struggling to be a sign of the inbreaking of God's rich kingdom of shalom.

13

The Descent of the Spirit

In the centre of the cloisters of Iona Abbey there stands an unusual and controversial bronze statue.

Called 'The Descent of the Spirit', it represents the Virgin Mary emerging from a vast heart formed by a canopy made of three parts of the sky and held up in the beak of a dove. The canopy is being brought to earth by three cherubs and received by a lamb. The back of the canopy carries on it the legend: 'Jacob Lipchitz, faithful to the religion of his ancestors, has made this Virgin for the better understanding of men on earth that the Spirit may reign.'

The sculpture was commissioned by Mrs Jane Owen of Texas, a descendant of Robert Owen, the first Scottish socialist who established a pioneering workers' co-operative at New Lanark. Very much influenced by the Iona Community, her 'New Harmony' community in the USA (complete with 'MacLeod Barn') expresses the hope of religious co-operation. Jacob Lipchitz, a practising Jew, made three identical bronze statues. Mrs Owen wished one to go to Iona, in recognition of the Celtic contribution to the idea of community — provided a Scots donor could put up £7,000 (in 1955). George MacLeod describes what happened.

> I well remember my reply (after a pause while I recovered my balance). I said, 'Madam, I do not know anyone in the world who would give £7,000 for any

cause: but if I did I would certainly seek it for the ongoing work of the Iona Community before any statue.'

She went sadly away, but returned the next morning to say that if I could find a donor of this statue for the Trustees, she would give £7,000 for the ongoing work of the Iona Community. Being human, I became even more interested in her proposition. But being sane, and ignorant in these things, I inquired more widely in the ensuing weeks into the intrinsic worth of the piece of sculpture. It was finally sufficient for me that Sir Kenneth Clark, a lover of Iona, a devoted son of Ardnamurchan and probably the greatest British authority on modern sculpture, commended the artist as quite outstanding and the statue as of lasting significance.

The statue was controversial because of its subject matter — the Virgin Mary — and its author — a Jew. When the gift was announced, there were dark hints about Roman Catholic take-overs, even though the eventual Scots donors — Sir John and Lady MacTaggart — were staunch Presbyterians as well as discerning art lovers. The statue itself sailed past Iona, in a cargo ship on the northern passage out of Poland and arrived on Scottish soil on Christmas Day, 1958.

'The Descent of the Spirit' in its central position at the heart of the Iona Abbey complex, stands as a symbol of the more universal dimension of the Iona Community's outreach, complementing the Scottish urban dimension. It is a statement in bronze of the Community's central theme: the invasion of the material by the spiritual, the Incarnation at the heart of the created order. It also links together, in its origins, the Old World and the New; and its inscription points towards a spiritual — material future transcending the old religious categories.

Set in the midst of a medieval abbey, this modern sign gathers up the ancient, still scandalous, theme of Incarnation and throws the imagination forward into the future. When George MacLeod first saw it, he saw the lineaments of an atomic bomb.

The Incarnation was indeed an inherent explosion into matter, setting up a chain reaction of igniting love that has sparked from heart to heart from that day to this and that one day will consume mankind in its lightsomeness or burning. The Celts called Christ 'the Sun behind all suns'. Ours is the first generation of mankind to know, not just upon our pulses but in our very text-books, that there is no such thing as dead matter. The very atom is best described as light-energy. And has not the Church taught down the centuries that Christ is the Light of the World and its Life (energy)?

If we reduce such phrases to the concept of a flickering candle in the dark, or merely a mystic spark within the soul, if we miss the 'many-splendoured thing', then quite simply we have mislaid the key for which the modern world is blindly groping. Men will look elsewhere — and vainly — for their salvation. We stand, if we care to enter, on the edge of the most spiritual age the world has ever known. Full acceptance of the Incarnation is the primary key to this atom as enlightenment and not explosion.

In a world in which not only the old but the modern categories are breaking down, the past-future motif of 'The Descent of the Spirit' feeds the imagination.

The modern scientific 'models', which have been so productive, are no longer up to the job. The news has not yet percolated down, and as a civilization we still carry on as if it were business as usual. We all operate with different 'models' of the world. A model is simply a way of seeing, an experiment, a frame, a working explanation. As children, we develop our model of the world, our own personal and unique world view. It is shaped by parents, friends, school, church, nation and community, as well as by our genes. The important thing about models is that they are provisional, they are the best we have at the time. They never incorporate all the evidence, they often distort — but they work. The models of the world we develop as children enable us to survive, they become habitual, second nature. We even fit the evidence into the model. As adults we very often live with an unchanged model of the world — one which is anachronistic and limiting but which, to a certain degree, still functions.

The scientific model which most of us have is a Newtonian one. It is a fixed-frame, cause-and-effect model of the universe: one thing causes another which causes another. The world is viewed as a machine and everything is measurable. The goal of science is to produce objective knowledge which will allow us to control this world.

Philosophically, we come under the dominating influence of Descartes ('I think, therefore I am'). He sought to reduce everything to its component parts. Only 'scientific' knowledge counted, and scientific knowledge was that which could be proved and measured and deduced.

The combined Newtonian-Cartesian model has been brilliantly successful in explaining many aspects of the world and cutting through much superstitious nonsense. Yet it has also been devastating: radical questioning, everything reduced to its basic elements; love reduced to chemical interactions; body and mind as separate units. Pushed to extremes, the dominant model has had horrific effects. What place is there for love or faith if you cannot define them, or you reduce them to other characteristics? This model has led to uncontrolled technology and the rape of the earth. It has led to viewing people as machines or rats in a maze. Marxist analysis, despite its strongly prophetic element, has followed mechanistic, historically-determined lines and become tyrannical (the end justifying the means). Freudian analysis, equally prophetic, has been mechanistic and reductionistic. Economics and politics have become detached from a total view of life and have produced dehumanizing distortions. Rampant capitalism and consumerism draw greedily from this infected well.

The dominant model has also been devastating for health. Along with science generally, it has had spectacular successes, but it has led inexorably to 'magic bullet' medicine, where the doctor prescribes a drug to deal with symptoms. The whole person is missing. Everything is cast into the problem/solution mould.

Modern technology has been the most impressive result, but it is a runaway technology, torn from any wider value system. The logical end of this road is high-tech nuclear horror.

In the meantime, there is a deep malaise, a sickening unto death. The cracks in the foundations are appearing, the flags of a new dawn are showing on the scientific battle front. Why? Because the dominant model is no longer adequate to deal with the new evidence. Scientists now work with a much more organic view of the world. Things are more provisional, free-flowing. 'Objective' and 'certain' are words more rarely used: relativity and uncertainty are built into every picture. The world is a more open system — or set of systems — than could ever have been realized before. In this exciting and fluid situation, the languages of science and of mysticism are no longer so divergent. Words such as 'mystery' and 'reverence' are no longer inappropriate to the modern scientific enterprise.

The revolution — for it is no less than this — is matched by growing questioning in the field of health care. The Cartesian split between mind and body is being seen for the disaster it is. The Indian yogis have known for centuries that the 'involuntary' systems of the body, such as heartbeat and blood pressure, can be influenced and even controlled by the mind; now, through the discipline of biofeedback, it is being demonstrated scientifically.

One of the most exciting areas of research is the study of the brain. The left hemisphere of the brain apparently handles rational thought, linear thinking, numbers, etc. The right side is involved with non-verbal thinking, pictures, art, synthesis, seeing things whole. A consequence of our being in thrall to the old model is that the left side of the brain has had the dominant role, and rational thinking has been much more highly valued than intuition. Linear thinking has been celebrated, dreams have been downgraded. Abstract thinking has been preferred to. The consequences of this unbalanced approach have been both spectacular and disastrous. Purely left hemisphere thinking may yet be the death of us all, as it leads inexorably to the terrifying logic of 'first strike' nuclear capability. The trouble with this kind of thinking based on technique is that it has no heart.

The implications of all of this are staggering. We live at a time when the dominant model of the age is disintegrating (yet this thinking is still part of the air we breathe, still feels natural even when it is distorted and distorting), and a new, more inclusive model has not yet been constructed. It is a dangerous, yet potentially exciting, time. When scientists talk about mystery, when theologians fall down manholes and humanists fall up Godholes, when doctors preach meditation and physicists talk about reverence, all the old categories are up for grabs. What we need is not to exchange one infallible model for another, but to find a balance: the left brain with the right brain, the male with the female, the Yin with the Yang, the East with the West, prayer with action. It is an open question as to whether we have the time or the will for such a cultural transformation.

Christianity may itself be transformed. It has been badly affected by the Newtonian-Cartesian frame: God has been pushed to the edges, to fill the few remaining gaps. He is either redundant, dead or relegated to the area of private spiritual experience. Bonhoeffer's dream of a life with God at the centre, at the strong points of life rather than shuffling around shadowy areas of weakness and inadequacy, may yet be realized.

There is new theological and practical work to be done. Prayer, for instance, is so often assumed to be a matter of words, words. When we have misinformed God about the state of half his world, we still feel inadequate because we have not prayed for the other half. There seems no way off that guilty treadmill. But if prayer can be a silent realization of the presence of God in whose life we live and move and have our being, a realization of wonder and mystery, then prayer becomes as natural as breathing. The material is shot through with the spiritual: there is a 'withinness' of God in all life. The whole earth is sacramental: every thing is truly every blessed thing, and it is indeed blasphemy to use the very atom to kill.

In this life of God, who is both cosmic lord and personal lover, we see how the personal and the corporate are indissolubly linked. Reverence for the earth, God's sacrament, is not only right and fitting, it is essential for the survival of the planet. So it is too with reverence for people, bearers also of the life of God. The image of man as dominant exploiter of the earth must be replaced by that of man as steward of God's creation, holding all things in trust.

For things which are 'second nature' to be displaced, a new awareness is required. Reverence for people and reverence for the earth are not new, but they are certainly radical. To become aware of the sacramental nature of the cosmos, to be open to the sacramental possibilities of each moment, to see the face of Christ in every person: these things are not novel, but their recovery is the beginning of our health.

We do not need to romanticize the Celts or to turn them all into saints to see that they have things to teach us about these matters.

> Be the eye of God betwixt me and each eye,
> The purpose of God betwixt me and each purpose,
> The hand of God betwixt me and each hand,
> The shield of God betwixt me and each shield,

The desire of God betwixt me and each desire,
The bridle of God betwixt me and each bridle,
And no mouth can curse me.

Be the pain of Christ betwixt me and each pain,
The love of Christ betwixt me and each love,
The dearness of Christ betwixt me and each
dearness,
The kindness of Christ betwixt me and each
kindness,
The wish of Christ betwixt me and each wish,
The will of Christ betwixt me and each will,
And no venom can wound me.

This prayer from Alexander Carmichael's collection *Carmina Gadelica* speaks of a Christ presence which is closer than breathing. But it is not a romantic world in which cheerful messages of peace and harmony will somehow bring in the reign of God. This kind of religious Utopianism was no use to the Celts and is equally futile today. Evil is not disposed of by positive thinking and holding hands.

Thou Mary of mildness,
Thou Mary of honour,
Succour me and shield me
With thy linen mantle,
With thy linen mantle.

Thou Christ of the trees,
Thou Christ of the cross,
Snatch me from the snares
Of the spiteful ones of evil,
The spiteful ones of evil.

Thou Father of the waifs,
Thou Father of the naked,
Draw me to the shelter-house
Of the saviour of the poor,
Of the saviour of the poor.

When Mother Teresa asked a number of school children in India where God was, the Christian children pointed 'up there' and the Hindu children pointed 'in here'. Incarnational Christian faith says that both answers are correct. God is the lord of the cosmos who is outraged over injustice; he is also the One whom we encounter in the depths of our being. Indian theology has retained a sense of the mystery at the heart of life. The God who is to be found in 'the cave of the heart' is not a domesticated pet.

Life is inescapably mysterious, even when we hold on to faith. Rationalistic Protestantism and jolly Catholicism try to do away with the mystery: everything is cut down to size, explained; God becomes the pal next door; language becomes too simple, too tame, incapable of bearing mystery; everything becomes functional, reductionist. And our hearts are empty.

People will beat a path to the holy man or woman who can point them to God. That, of course, has its dangers, particularly when credulous youth meets cynical manipulative religion.

One of Iona's gifts has been to help ordinary people form a language which speaks of vocation in simple terms — a vocabulary which is at the same time rich and responsive to mystery, yet accessible to the non-academic believer. Even so, the task of forming an earthy spirituality which is appropriate to busy lives and tenement closes is still in its infancy, as is the job of shaping a new worship which is both simple and mysterious and speaks to right brain and left brain, heart and head. The worthy wordiness of rationalistic religion and immobile, word-based services do not touch people at enough points.

Iona Abbey, with its Hebridean strength, colour, sense of history and explorations in worship which take the contemporary world seriously, appeals to a very wide range of people. Yet the most significant factor is that the worship springs from the life of a living community. Worship can only be renewed as the life of the Christian community is renewed.

What requires to be reshaped is a total gospel for the total human being. Iona has always represented a searching for comprehensive expressions of the faith, arising out of community. One contemporary sign of this is to be found in the healing ministry of the Iona Community. The laying-on of hands is not exercised by one person, but by the whole community — and the leader of worship kneels to receive the hands of the community (just as, in the Community's morning office, the leader of worship confesses his or her sins and hears the absolution pronounced by the whole congregation). Nor is the laying-on of hands seen as a separate 'religious' activity — it is part of the totality of healing which is both 'in here' in the person and 'out there' in the world.

Christianity itself needs to be healed. Paraded as a conquering ideology within a privileged 'Christendom', it has been obsessed with power and order. In the face of a world ravaged by injustice and moving towards the brink of nuclear holocaust, the Church's obsession with who is in and who is out, who can and cannot celebrate and receive communion, and other equally riveting ecclesiastical matters, is quite indecent. Christianity, while proclaiming unity, has been a source of deep division. Yet the source of its healing is embedded in its own heart. The Indian theologian M. M. Thomas observes wisely that the Church is defined by its centre, Jesus Christ, and not by its circumference.

The Incarnation is a specific time- and space-bound sign which is yet open to the future. It may be that Christian faith, welcoming the hard-won insights of other religious traditions, will make a transforming leap comparable with the shift from an exclusively Jewish to a world-wide faith. At our heart is Jesus Christ, divine and human, who is surely at the root of today's divine-human explosion. The transformation of our world into a place of peace and justice requires such a radical change in consciousness.

The Iona Virgin, set with wonderful irony in the heart of the old masculine bastion, points us to a person who is neglected and feared by left-brained Protestantism and exalted into a pseudo-goddess cum anti-sex symbol by the unhealthy wing of Catholicism. Mary needs to be liberated from the grisly hang-ups and defensive positions of centuries, to be revealed as what the biblical tradition shows her to be: the person who *par excellence* opened herself in lowliness to One who brings new life out of acknowledged impotence.

Our Lady of Iona is pregnant with possibilities.

14

Dancing with a Limp

The mortality rate among religious communities is notoriously high. Some die stillborn. Others have serious accidents during adolescence. Still others find that symptoms of lassitude turn into a midlife crisis which is suddenly terminal.

Religious communities are vulnerable because they live on the edge, both spiritually and financially. They are formed to meet a need, and they usually do that with intensity for some years. When the need is met, or the agenda shifts, or the leadership changes, or the community fails to adapt, disintegration sets in. Most communities are founded by charismatic leaders, and the intensity of their life and the provisional nature of their organization contrasts with the institutional Church, which is organized for the long haul. Some communities manage to continue even though they actually died years ago. Others are suddenly blown away by inflationary winds which expose the perilous economic foundations of the group.

Simply to exist for half a century is an achievement. To go beyond dependence on a founding father and renew its purposes is no small thing. But does the Iona Community have a future, and if so, what kind of future?

In its early days, the Iona Community had a maxim, 'The movement is a work of faith. It will continue just as long as God requires it.' Now this may be a somewhat messianic motto, but it has the virtue of recognizing the essentially provisional nature of the Iona Community: it is a disposable tool, not an everlasting institution; it is only a tiny part of the Church's witness. Even if the Community were to self-destruct tomorrow, God would somehow manage to struggle through His day.

In order to remain a living organism, a community needs both continuity and discontinuity. The problem in such cases is to discern what is fundamental and what needs to change. It is easy to get it wrong, as the history of movements within the Church will show. Some monastic orders were locked into their own past and became fossilized. Others, in the heady post-Vatican II atmosphere, jumped the convent wall, exchanged traditional habits for miniskirts and swapped the language of the liturgy for the language of the encounter group. Their illness was shorter, but just as terminal.

The Iona Community is old enough to have a history. For many of its members today, the rebuilding of the Abbey is simply a story. It would be possible to be an Iona Community fundamentalist: to live in a nostalgic *dwam* (an emotional sea in one's head) and meditate on a Golden Age; to stay with the Iona Community equivalent of the Tridentine Mass. The trouble is that the Golden Age was indeed heroic but also — as we have seen — messy, full of argument, tension and indecision as well as sacrifice and vision. To romanticize the early days of the Iona Community would be about as helpful as romanticizing the Early Church. The other temptation is to throw over history, declare it redundant and talk only in the present tense.

A sense of continuity is needed if the Iona Community is to retain its identity. It is impossible to talk about the Iona Community without telling a story which has its origins in sixth-century Ireland and twentieth-century Glasgow. Silence here would cause the very stones of Iona Abbey to shout aloud. Yet the Community cannot live by stories alone, however engrossing or inspiring, and nor has it tried to do so. The Community has had to adapt to the major changes caused by the end of the rebuilding and the retirement of its founder. In the late 1970s it had to ask serious questions about its continued existence and the affirmative response was accompanied by a redefinition of its purposes and a reshaping of its organization for the next decade. The numbers of Members and Associates joining, the continued appeal of the developing Iona programme and the response to its mainland work would seem to indicate that if the Iona Community were to disband today it would need to be reinvented tomorrow.

To predict the future of the Iona Community would be a perilous and not terribly useful enterprise. As we have seen, the most profound changes in the life of the Community have come unbidden and unplanned. The Wild Goose is not a domesticated pet. It would be more profitable to ask the question: what are the elements in the Iona story which can be retained and adapted to serve the needs of the future?

As the Community has evolved and been made to review its beliefs and practices, these are questions that have had to be asked at different stages. In 1977 Ralph Morton wrote that the Iona Community was

> 'no longer an experiment but a community with a life
> of its own. It is like a family. So long as a family is
> made up of living people and they are bound together
> by a common way of life and have a place to live in or
> to come back to, it continues as a visible, effective
> social unit. Without these assets, it disappears. And
> families do disappear.'

Dr Morton identified the Community's assets as the continuity of its membership, the experience that underlies their attitudes and a place that is their own.

The membership of the Iona Community is certainly what makes it unique. When one asks the question, 'What does the Iona Community do?' the answer turns out to be complex. Obviously part of the answer is to point to the corporate work on Iona, at Camas and on the mainland which is very visible. Yet the work of each member in many different situations and locations is equally important. And the work of the 'front line' is extended by fourteen hundred Associates with an ever widening circle of interests and commitments.

The membership is ever-changing, yet there is continuity. To read the historical documents of the Community is to be reminded of the large numbers of people who have at one time been members. The fact that each member has to make a positive decision to 'sign in' each year has led to a healthy regular turnover. Few members leave for ideological reasons — it is generally because of extended commitments elsewhere. The Community encourages members to look at their priorities each year, and a decision to resign — always checked out with family groups — is not regarded as a failure. This continual movement has prevented stagnation, and the regular influx of new members has brought fresh questioning and new ideas. The Iona Community is a close family, but never a closed one.

The more recent upsurge in membership has brought both problems and opportunities. Is there a magic number at which a group ceases to be a community in any meaningful sense of the word? The Iona Community has declined to fix a ceiling, but it is a continuing issue. It is compounded by the geographical spread and diverse religious allegiance of the new members, prompting the question whether the Iona Community still has a predominantly Scottish identity. In 1987 the Community had its first-ever plenary meeting outside Scotland, at York. However, the particular place the Iona Community holds in Scottish life and the geographical influence of Iona and Glasgow are not matters of mere sentiment. They are matters of fact and responsibility, part of a particular tapestry which could not be unravelled without consequent loss of identity. Being rooted in Scotland is not the opposite of internationalism. The Community's incarnational stress means that it is time- and space-bound in ways that are both limiting and expansive. It is not a free-floating, ethereal club. The diversity of interests represented within the Community also raises questions about the extent to which it can still be considered a church movement. Or is it even an alternative church?

In 1938 the issue was clearcut. The Iona Community was training ordained men for the institutional Church and indeed for a particular church, the Church of Scotland. There was confidence that the institutional Church was the proper place in which to concentrate energy and resources. For some people today, the Iona Community functions as an alternative church, even though this is not a role which the Community has sought.

We are made aware daily of how much the Community means to so many people. There are countless people, both within the traditional Church and far outside it, who hang on to faith by their fingernails, and Iona provides a ledge, a sanctuary and a light. There are people hanging on to that ledge who would find no place within the existing churches. The Iona Community needs to remain committed to the Church in both its institutional and alternative senses: to ride both horses in the ring simply because both horses have a right to be there. It is one of the unique functions of religious communities to do precisely that.

The question before us is not whether we can live without

institutions, but whether our institutions can be renewed. Most of us owe our faith to the institutional Church, with all its sins and follies and glories. Amidst the congregations are people of all kinds trying to live out the Gospel. If we believe in incarnated faith, we must take the Church seriously. The Iona Community is not an unrooted spiritual free-floating Utopian association of dreamers, but a community of believers rooted in the life of the earthly, visible Church. Yet we need broader definitions of the Church than are presently on offer — the maxim about the Church being defined by its centre rather than by its circumference will do for starters — and until such definitions are not only articulated but lived out, the role of groups like the Iona Community will be to keep people 'hanging in' and talking with each other.

The issue of ecclesiastical institutions is closely related to that of political institutions. As with the Church, many people have abandoned political institutions, preferring to concentrate on single-issue politics or life style questions. This trend has been reflected in the Iona Community. Crusading and acting on single issues has been creative and produced uncharacteristic coalitions of interest groups. There is justification for the lack of confidence in the traditional political processes, but at the end of the day, concentration on single-issue politics bypasses the crucial problems of political power. If concerns about peace and justice are to be incarnated, the process of political change needs to be taken more seriously. There is room in the Iona Community both for party-political commitment and for 'alternative' struggles — again, both horses are properly in the ring — but the reshaping rather than the abandonment of political institutions has to be central to the dialogue if wishful thinking is not to replace reality. The Community has always feared analysis paralysis, but a sharper critique of political power, from the particular angle of the poor, is required for its future work.

The critique needs to be part of a recommitment to 'apprenticeships in difficult places', and God's bias to the poor. Since the Community stopped using its hands to build a building, its commitment to the urban scene has become more diffuse. Yet in the 1980s the Youth Volunteer scheme, the Columban Houses, Walter Fyfe's work in the Gorbals and the Peregrini scheme provided pointers towards the shape of the next stage of the Community's urban commitment. They represent lay, rather than ordained, ventures, in keeping with the Community's thrust in recent years.

The equipping of the whole people of God is one of the critical issues facing the world Church. The Church is a movement which operates at a fraction of its full potential. The dominant role of professional clergy and the consequent dependent attitude of many people in the pews — often people used to taking responsibility in other areas of their lives — has contributed to this wasteful state of affairs. How is this to be rectified? It is often assumed that changes have to be made 'at the top', and that these will 'trickle down'. This assumption is as debatable as the belief that the wealth of the rich will somehow benefit the poor. The trouble with decisions made at the top is that they emerge from a particular world view, training and agenda, and do not usually come out of a process of listening and partnership.

The ferment among the laity in the Roman Catholic Church is an encouraging sign — and we have seen evidence of it on Iona — as is the formation of base Christian communities in Latin America and Europe. Ian Fraser, a senior member of the Iona Community who is one of the foremost authorities on these movements, has documented trends which indicate the struggles for new birth which are going on. A church of the people rather than for the people reflects the dynamism of the central Reformed doctrine of 'the priesthood of all believers' — a doctrine which is potentially revolutionary but which is kept under lock and key and only allowed out in the company of a professional trusty.

The formation of a servant Church which is 'owned' by all its people is a formidable but exciting enterprise. The Iona Community, which is still in the process of moving from being an ordained movement into which lay people fit, to a genuine partnership of lay and ordained, women and men, is one possible handmaiden for such a Church. The task of the equipping of the people of God must start where the people are, not where professionals would like them to be. The Peregrini programme, starting with the skills, talents and commitment of two unemployed young people, convinced the Community of the need for experiment in a variety of models of training for various ministries within and outwith the traditional Church. Iona Abbey, Camas and the new MacLeod Centre, linked to the Columban Houses and projects of members on the mainland, can be seen as a moveable campus in a university of vocations, as the search continues for models which could be used by the Church at large in its task of mobilizing the whole people of God. Professional, ordained ministry should find its proper servant role in such a lively context. This is particularly critical at a time when shortage of ordained ministers is leading the Church to form bigger and bigger amalgamations, rather than encouraging small congregations to come up with solutions which do not require a resident professional. What is seen as a tragedy and a crisis should be viewed as an opportunity for radical and positive change.

Groups like the Iona Community — ecumenical, travelling light, maverick, and able to make quick decisions, have a particular role within the Church. The danger for such groups is that they will be co-opted by a benign establishment and become toothless pet bears. The other temptation is to stray too near to the edge of nuttiness — radical and innovative ideas, discussed by enthusiasts in an intense atmosphere which is light years away from the concerns of ordinary people can do strange things to otherwise nice people.

One of the factors which roots the Iona Community in the soil of reality is its responsibility for Iona Abbey. There have been times in the life of the Community when the Abbey has been felt to be more of a burden than a blessing. The continual living on a financial knife-edge in order to keep the costs down for ordinary people, and the sheer amount of energy which goes into running the Abbey have tempted members from time to time to suggest pulling out and concentrating on one particular mainland activity. The Community could easily have become a rather élitist urban sect, with the initiates sharing a common specialist language.

There would be plenty of takers for Iona Abbey. It might be turned into a conventional retreat centre, or could be a very profitable enterprise, catering for wealthy people seeking spiritual saunas. What would be missed would be that unique blend of worship and work in the context of shared Christian community — an experience accessible to all people, no matter what their background.

The incessant questions and demands and insights of those pilgrims has shaped the Iona Community in unenvisaged ways and compelled the Community to deal with the concerns of ordinary people. At times when it has wanted to pursue one narrow line, the seekers have forced the Community to respond in broader, more human terms. At other times, when the Community has wanted to concentrate on its own internal problems, its international constituency has hammered on the doors and made the Community face outwards. And the practicalities of everyday living on an island have fostered a healthy scepticism about global ideology.

The combination of historic Iona Abbey and the purpose-built modern MacLeod Centre, on one of the most inspiring sites in Europe, represents Christian resources of the highest order. In stewarding these resources, the Iona Community is itself inevitably transformed, and will continue to be transformed. It is a privileged work.

The island resources are inextricably linked to the Iona Community's greatest resource — people. The Community's members, Associates, Friends and wellwishers form a network of caring people living in many different kinds of situation in the world. They represent the cutting edge of the Community's mainland work and they also keep the Community grounded in reality. How best to support that frontline is a crucial question for the Iona Community, particularly as the shape of the task shifts in today's high-tech world of rapid and bewildering change. Answers from the 1930s or even the 1970s will not do, but the story, principles and experience of the Iona Community, filtered through the inspiration and life of Iona, can contribute towards the reshaping of new answers. Use the light you have, and pray for more light.

The future of the Iona Community is not assured, nor should it ever be. Adventure, rather than security, must be the name of its game. Wisdom without risk turns stale. At its worst, it degenerates into prudential mottos and arid nostalgia. Plenaries become Presbyteries, and the Wild Goose becomes a regularly dusted enamel plaque on a million suburban living room walls.

At a time when imperial, dominant forms of Christianity are thankfully collapsing, intentional religious communities like Iona may have a unique role in forging a new vocabulary and style for the Christian life. As the cracks in the foundations of the old permissive society grow wider and the stench of death grows stronger, there is a real danger of a reaction in favour of totalitarian religion and politics, driving out one set of demons and replacing them with another. The electronic church, the creepy television salesmen with the welded-on smiles, and the cults peddling instant salvation and success without tears, may make all the running.

The story of Jacob being wounded by the angel of God should inform us that meeting God may sometimes be more like being mugged by a mysterious stranger (or dive-bombed by a strangely persistent wild bird) than a sweet, sweet encounter with an indulgent Father. As people wounded in the struggle with God, we dance — but with a limp! (How did we ever give people the impression that the whole thing was about walking straight?)

After fifty years, the Iona Community's limp is pretty pronounced. But the dance — the dance goes on!

Epilogue

They still come, the long procession of the walking and sometimes dancing wounded, the living and the dying.

Even the dead have tried to make it. In 1985 it was finally decided that the corpse of an Oklahoma man, held in deep freeze for two years pending a decision, could not be buried in the sacred soil of Iona. He had wanted to sleep with the kings until the last trump wakened them all.

The extraordinary power of attraction of Iona is not simply an ancient memory. Sir Kenneth Clark in his television series, *Civilization*, observed:

> I never come to Iona — and I used to come here almost every year when I was young — without the feeling that 'some God is in this place'. It isn't as awe-inspiring as some other holy places — Delphi or Assisi. But Iona gives one more than anywhere else I know a sense of peace and inner freedom. What does it? The light, which floods round on every side? The lie of the land which, coming after the solemn hills of Mull, seems strangely like Greece, like Delos, even? The combination of wine-dark sea, white sand and pink granite? Or is it the memory of those holy men who for two centuries kept Western civilization alive?

The holiness of Iona lies in the people, not all of them saints by any means. The story of a very few is told in these pages. The bulk of the story — untold and unsung — is to be traced in Glasgow, in London, in Calcutta, and wherever the Wild Goose flies.

Yes, and still they come, though in ferries rather than coracles. Today's pace is a bit more frantic than that of the days of Columba.

As we look towards a new millennium, our pilgrimage cannot be a gentle amble. It is a chase. It can never be other than an ambiguous journey, despite precious moments of certainty and luminous clarity. We may still be wrong. It is inevitably a Wild Goose chase.

And the wild claim is that within that sacred Chase, the clues to our true destiny are to be found. Patrick Kavanagh says it beautifully:

> Then I saw the wild geese flying
> In fair formation to their bases in Inchicore
> And I knew that these wings would outwear
> the wings of war
> And a man's simple thoughts outlive
> the day's loud lying.
> Don't fear, don't fear, I said to my soul.
> The Bedlam of Time is an empty bucket rattled,
> 'Tis you who will say in the end who best battles.
> Only they who fly home to God have flown at all.

Postscript:
The Chase Continues!

The first edition of *Chasing the Wild Goose* was published to coincide with the Iona Community's fiftieth anniversary and the opening of the MacLeod Centre in August 1988; and Ron Ferguson's preface is dated St Columba's Day 1987. Now, ten years on, St Columba's Day 1997 is just past, the fourteen hundredth anniversary of his death, marked by a joyful concentration of special events — pilgrimages to Iona by groups of all denominations, yachts and coracles from Ireland, the celebration of Columba's life in music and drama, and a much-appreciated visit by President Mary Robinson of Ireland.

It has been an opportunity, much pursued through the media as well as by the Iona Community, to explore the significance of Columba for his time and ours, to correct some of the misunderstandings as to what constitutes 'Celtic spirituality', so fashionable these days, and to reflect also on what has been happening over these past ten years within the life of the Iona Community itself. (And any account such as this is inevitably impressionistic, too close to the events to be either dispassionate or factually comprehensive.)

The opening of the MacLeod Centre itself was so memorable, a satisfying completion of much effort by so many people — the fund-raising team of Ron Ferguson himself, Alison MacDonald, and Maxwell MacLeod; Ian Galloway, who had virtually been a clerk of works on top of his responsibilities as joint Abbey Warden; all the marathon runners; the participants in the 'Greatest Jumble Sale in the World', and those who had contributed in so many ways big and small. It was a grey day, but the singing and sense of occasion were abated neither by the weather nor by the dark and noisy presence of Pastor Jack Glass, protesting at the Community's continuing ecumenical commitment. The official opening was performed by Mrs Leah Tutu, wife of the Archbishop of Cape Town, who entered enthusiastically into the spirit of the proceedings; and George MacLeod clearly enjoyed the day immensely. Later in the week the Community expressed its thanks at the end of Ron Ferguson's leadership with a blend of fun and deep feeling that somehow reflected the spirit of the preceding years and sent him, leaning on a golden zimmer, on his way that would lead, via several highly acclaimed books (a biography of George MacLeod, and *Black Diamonds and the Blue Brazil* — reflections on Cowdenbeath and its football team), to his becoming minister of St Magnus Cathedral in Kirkwall, Orkney, where he has continued to write regular newspaper columns and, most recently, a very well-received spectacular dramatic and musical event, based on the Orkney sagas, that had its premiere at the 1997 St Magnus Festival.

Ron Ferguson was succeeded as Leader of the Community by John Harvey, coincidentally at the time his next door neighbour as minister of Govan Old Parish Church, from which George MacLeod had founded the Community fifty years earlier. John had worked for some years in the 1960s with the Gorbals Group, an experience that had significantly shaped his understanding of the mission of the Church and the priorities of the needs of those who are disadvantaged. From there he had gone with his family to Iona as Abbey Warden to establish, with the encouragement of Ian Reid as Leader at the time, the arrangement that the Community's island centres have run on ever since, with a core of resident staff, shorter-term volunteers, and guests 'sharing the common life' week by week. John in turn was succeeded as Leader by myself in 1995, coming from a rather different background, first in the civil service and then in university chaplaincy work and teaching, but with a common interest in the mission of the Church today and in the social and political implications of the Gospel — and we are brothers-in-law (our wives' parents having met while working with George MacLeod in Govan in the 1930s!).

In reflecting on these past ten years memory is inevitably selective, and it is interesting and instructive to sift through some of the Community's publications and other papers to help fill the gaps. There have been surprises and disappointments, high points alongside times that were not quite so good, continuing themes and trends as well as significant changes. The death of George MacLeod in 1991 was of course a huge landmark, and both the funeral in June and the memorial service at Govan in September were unforgettable occasions. It was a great joy to the Community that George in 1989 was awarded the international Templeton Prize for Progress in Religion; characteristically, he decided that half should be used immediately for the relief of the needs of the hungry and the other half invested with the income to be used to support the Community's work for justice and peace. And in February 1997 Ian Reid died, George's successor as Leader from 1967 to 1974, so much loved and respected also for his pastoral and organizational gifts, and for the ministry of prayer and correspondence he had continued to fulfil even when his mobility was latterly severely reduced.

The Community has grown over recent years — grown both as a movement and an organization. Although the membership of the Community has remained fairly steady at just over two hundred for several years there are signs now that it is increasing, with more people seeking to become Members than the new members' programme can accommodate; and the wider constituency of Associate Members and Friends is expanding also. The interest in the Community's work and concerns seems as strong as ever, reflected both in the numbers coming to Iona (running now at more than 1200 a day in high summer, over 160,000 in 1996) and seeking to stay for the week's programme in the Community's island centres, and in the demand for the services of the Community's Wild Goose Resource Group, the books and worship material published by the Community and general information about the Community.

With the opening of the MacLeod Centre the staff complement on Iona has increased considerably (standing now at just over twenty on one- or three-year contracts, along with up to thirty volunteers). Some of the more specialized jobs have been more difficult to fill from time to time, and the pace and intensity of life is extremely demanding. But as with the guests, where the community that is formed among staff involves a range of different national backgrounds and ages, the experience tends to be enriching for all. The Community is fortunate in having had a succession of gifted and committed

Wardens who have left their own distinctive stamp on the islands work through the contribution they have made — Alison and Philip Newell, Lynda Wright, Christian MacLean, Joanna Anderson, Donald Scott, Adrian Rennie and, currently, Peter Millar, not forgetting the continuing valued work of Dafydd Owen as Director of the MacLeod Centre.

Many people are still unaware of the dispersed character of the Community. They understandably assume that the resident group on Iona are 'the Iona Community', and are surprised to learn of the scale of the mainland headquarters at the Pearce Institute in the heart of Govan where the Community began. Here too the operation and activities have expanded and there have been certain significant changes. Projects have stopped as well as started as circumstances have determined; for example, the Peregrini (lay-training) scheme ended, owing to lack of demand, in 1990; Helen Steven's remit as peace and justice worker was adjusted, through an arrangement, jointly funded with the Quakers, for her to be located at, and work from, Peace House at Greenloaning in Perthshire; Centrepeace, the Third World shop and resource centre in Glasgow, which the Community had strongly supported since it opened in the early 1980s, closed in 1994 owing to financial difficulties; and two outreach workers (Christine Reid and Kathy Galloway) were employed, mostly in the local community in and around Govan, for a few years. But with the basic turnover rising strikingly (almost £1.2m in 1996) the need for adequate administrative and financial support has been clear and key new posts were created (company secretary in 1989 and support services manager in 1992) to relieve the general burden on the Leader and release him for wider strategic tasks.

Alongside this there has been considerable expansion in both the staffing and output of Wild Goose Publications and the work of the Wild Goose Worship and Resource Groups, whose 'well deserved reputation' (as Dr Ian Bradley puts it in his book *Columba, pilgrim and penitent*, specially commissioned for the fourteen hundredth anniversary) 'for innovative and creative liturgical reform takes its members into churches the length and breadth of the British Isles and beyond to enthuse congregations and lead worship workshops'. For many people the Wild Goose Resource Group (the present members are Alison Adam, John Bell, Graham Maule, and Mairi Munro) are 'the Iona Community' and the valuable contribution that they make to the life of the Community and the wider Church through seeking to shape and create new forms of relevant, participative worship has been reflected both in the generous grant the Church of Scotland has made towards their work for several years and in the Community's decision in 1996 to 'core-fund' them. Similarly the Community has indicated the importance it attaches to youth work by adopting a new youth policy in 1991, reviving the category of Youth Associates in 1995 to meet the wishes of young people to be more closely involved with the life of the Community, and paying its youth development worker (Ruth Clements succeeded Alison Adam in 1995) for several years from 'core funds' rather than, as for some years previously, from specially raised project income.

Some of these changes have been the results not so much of shifting priorities as of what the Community can afford. For some years now the Community's finances have been relatively healthy, but there is a sense still, particularly when a significant amount of trading income is involved, that there is something intrinsically fragile and precarious about our existence. Yes, we have grown; yes, we have recently reorganized and attempted to streamline our decision-making processes by distinguishing more clearly between strategic policy and what can be left to management; yes, we have introduced staff training and other procedures appropriate to an organization with the scale and scope of ours. But there is still a strong feeling of living on the edge of risk; and this is perhaps how it should be.

On a recent visit to Scotland, Jean Vanier, founder of L'Arche Community, discussed the growth of his own organization and the need to retain its prophetic cuttting-edge and readiness to take risks, as intrinsic to its commitment to the Gospel. The Iona Community shares this dilemma among the issues it faces at present. On the one hand we are immensely encouraged that there appears to be so much interest in and support for what we are offering and doing in our work on both Iona and the mainland. On the other hand it is important that we should continue to challenge one another, challenge the churches, challenge our political leaders — not simply for the sake of challenging, but because fundamental to the Christian vocation and perspective is a perpetual discontent and restlessness with the prevailing culture and consciousness, with the way things are when measured alongside the purposes of God, the vision and values of God's kingdom, expressed in terms of justice, love, peace, and fullness of life.

For almost thirty years from its inception the Community was about building — the restoration of the living quarters of the Benedictine Abbey. Then in the 1980s we built the MacLeod Centre, and in the early 1990s we built Cul-Shuna, accommodation for our volunteers behind the village street on Iona. Sometimes it is easier to express the basic purpose of the Community when it has a visible or tangible sign. But I firmly believe that we are still about rebuilding. We are about rebuilding the lives of individuals — with our deep concern for healing, our recognition of the brokenness of the lives of each one of us, as our morning prayer says, and our awareness that so many people in today's world are looking for depth, purpose and meaning in their lives. We are about the rebuilding of the Church — a concern of the Community at the outset which we perhaps need to recover as a priority of the Community today, when at all levels the Church appears to struggle to survive and, with declining numbers and confidence, increasingly turns in on itself rather than reach out in recognition that life is to be found through being ready to give it away. We are also about the rebuilding of society, seeing this too as part of our mission to seek, explore and discover 'new ways to touch the hearts of all' as one of our Community prayers puts it; and this is why action for peace and justice is a key part of the Rule to which Members are committed and why for so many of us political involvement, working for social change, and campaigning on issues at both local and national level are such a priority.

The church environment is changing, and not just negatively, because there are many signs of hope and growth. We continue to emphasize that the Iona Community is not a substitute for local church involvement; and over these past years we have strengthened our links with the official church structures, for instance the Iona Community Board (the connection with the Church of Scotland created in 1951) has since 1993 contained representatives of the other main denominations from which the Community draws its membership, and we are formally associated with the ecumenical bodies for Britain (CCBI), Scotland (ACTS) and England. We are committed to improving mutual understanding among the denominations, as well as promoting inter-faith dialogue, and to working towards fuller eucharistic sharing: in this connection, following consultations on Iona in 1993 and 1995, an initiative was taken to launch a petition, 'Call for 2000', seeking the possibility of sharing Communion at ecumenical centres and events where people were sharing so many other aspects of their lives; the petition attracted an encouraging response, was formally presented at the second European Ecumenical Assembly at Graz, Austria in June 1997 and is now being followed up. Our belonging within the world-wide Church is consistently reflected in the Community's intercessory prayers on Iona and elsewhere, the international character of our staff group on Iona (often drawn from as many as five continents) as well as our wider constituency of Associates and Friends, and our commitment to world issues. Indeed it is the Community's holding together of spiritual and social concerns, the expression of this through worship, and the attempt to embody it within the structure and thrust of our life together that is perhaps distinctive and appears to attract so much interest. It is one thing to experience and sustain this on Iona, whether for a week or a season; it is something else altogether to reflect this within the continuing life of a multi-faceted local congregation. Those who have an enriching time on Iona are often frustrated and disappointed that the experience apparently cannot be reproduced in their local situation; of course the context is not at all the same and the challenge is to apply and adapt the insights in ways that are appropriate to a different setting.

And there have been dramatic changes too in the backcloth against which the Community has been pursuing its political concerns and priorities — most notably perhaps, the fall of the Berlin Wall, the end of apartheid in South Africa, the Gulf War and the General Election of 1997, hailed in some quarters as the dawning of a new era, following the rout of the Conservatives in what was seen by some as a reaction to the injustices caused by the dominance of market-driven ideology, by others (who perhaps saw a greater degree of convergence in the main parties' policies) as the result simply of a desire for change.

In 1989 the Community drew up what was rather grandiosely described as a 'strategic plan'; this adjusted certain aspects of the organizational structure but was helpful also in identifying, and committing the Community corporately to pursuing, specific working priorities. The intention was that each member would be associated with a particular 'area of concern', which would be carried forward through working groups. In practice, as with so much else within the life of the Community (and this is perhaps as it should be, since uniformity of structure is more likely to be a straitjacket than a channel of creativity), this has worked rather unevenly: in most cases there is a small working group of up to ten Members (sometimes involving some Associates also) and a wider group of interested people who keep in touch mainly through correspondence. There has continued to be a special concern about racism, and the Community has been instrumental in the creation of the organization Christians Action for Justice in Immigration Law (CAJIL) and active in opposing recent legislation which increased restrictions and controls on immigrants and asylum-seekers. Another priority was identified as the cause of the poor and the exploited, and representatives of the Community have shared in many initiatives, at both local and national level, which seek to combat and draw attention to poverty and injustice, give a voice to those who are not normally heard and work for political change. There has also been continuing involvement in the campaign for nuclear disarmament — against Trident in particular — a commitment to non-violence and the role of the United Nations, the support of ethical investment and 'the new economics', the pursuit of a range of environmental concerns, and association with moves towards constitutional change — the creation of a Scottish Parliament and regional assemblies in England, relations with the European Union and electoral reform. On all these matters the question of communication is at issue: while inevitably only a few Members will be involved in any particular topic event, it is essential that the membership at large should be kept informed, and it has not always proved possible to achieve this satisfactorily. Also it is important to say that, in this whole area of social and political change, the Community will very seldom be acting alone; sometimes the Community may initiate action and seek to involve other groups; in other cases the Community may join a coalition that is already formed. In all cases the object is to avoid duplication and to recognize the strength of concerted action and the significance of the new political culture that is gradually emerging, the movement of 'civil society' founded in flexible alliances of like-minded bodies and groups that come together to pursue common causes.

The Community completed a three year review of its 'strategic plan' in 1996. This experience produced a salutary recognition of the significance of giving as much attention to process as to content; and this is likely to be a continuing emphasis over the next few years — the balancing of the contemplative and the activist, of which the cat and the monkey on either side of the window on the south wall of the Abbey keep reminding us, the need for a community which is largely made up of strong-minded workoholics (Ian Reid referred to the difficulty as Leader of trying to control a hundred and forty wild horses pulling in different directions — and now there are more than two hundred!) to find time also for a more reflective mode of being. The growth and composition of the Community presents its own challenges, not only in terms of structures and formal processes, but also in how we sustain and develop our belonging together. There are now almost as many women as men within the membership; and there are more lay people than ordained. Although the Church of Scotland is still the dominant denomination, there are Members from all the main churches in Britain and, with one third of the twenty-seven Members' Family Groups in England, and a significant number of New Members in recent years coming from England, the centre of gravity may be shifting: while Iona, and the concerns and commitment it expresses, will remain at the heart of the Community's life, it can no longer be assumed that what are essentially Scottish, or Church of Scotland, concerns are shared by all. The diversity of background and experience is a tremendous enrichment and source of strength; the challenge lies in how to harness and direct it, in developing a style of life, a creative process that enables us to relate closely to and sustain one another despite the differences and the distances. The Iona Community, as we keep telling ourselves, is not just a loose association of kindred spirits with a vague commitment to certain slightly radical causes. Our accountability to one another, our common responsibility and readiness to own and be involved in what is done corporately is fundamental to our life together. And the sense of wider belonging together, within the broader constituency which also includes Associates and Friends and has been considerably strengthened over recent years, needs to be developed further, not only to reflect and harness the enthusiasm and commitment that is evident in the network of Iona groups that exists especially throughout England (and in parts of certain countries overseas also — Germany, Australia, and the United States at present) but also to fulfil more effectively the Community's responsibility towards those whose support and encouragement we value so much but who are perhaps looking to us for more than we are providing — and indeed, given the limitation on resources, can provide.

The recent developments in the Community's islands work, following the opening of the MacLeod Centre, have already been mentioned. The future of the work at Camas was a continuing focus of discussion, particularly after the change in 1989 to running the centre on a seasonal basis rather than through a resident staff group. In 1995 the Community approved plans to put Camas on a more secure footing through the appointment of a three-year team leader, with support staff qualified in outdoor pursuits, and the commitment of funds to improve the facilities and carry out necessary buildings work.

The level of bookings at Camas, as at the Abbey and the MacLeod Centre, has been very encouraging over the last few years. It is always difficult to strike a balance between groups and individuals wanting to make a return visit and those seeking to come for the first time; and some people, especially from overseas, who understandably want to settle arrangements as early as possible, find it hard to accept that bookings are not taken more than a few months in advance! Since its opening, and rather contrary to the original intention, the programme at the MacLeod Centre had developed on broadly similar lines to what was offered at the Abbey, and in recent years efforts have been made to provide a different kind of shared experience, with a particular emphasis on young people and families.

Very often it is tempting, in the preoccupation with the Community's own work, to forget the significance of the local context. There is no denying that there have been times of tension in the past, and the books of Dr E. Mairi MacArthur, particularly *Columba's Island*, explore the history and sociology of Iona and discuss the Iona Community from the islanders' perspective. For the most part, however, relations with the island community have been good in recent years and there are opportunities, particularly during the quieter winter months, for the resident staff to strengthen the links. The coming together through special events is a beneficial process — whether these are local meetings about future developments (the National Trust's plans for the island; talk of a causeway or 'fixed-link' across the Sound of Mull); social occasions like the Community's annual Hallowing Service and supper, the local community's play in the Nunnery each summer, or an Abbey open day; or funerals, like the memorable thanksgiving in 1989 for the life of 'Doodie' MacFadyen, a much-loved local crofter, or the burial of John Smith, the Labour leader, in 1994. There are other areas of continuing sensitivity too — concerning, for example, the opening in 1996 of the new Roman Catholic retreat house, the Hillock of the Dove, and the need to establish a mutual trust that recognizes the Community's ecumenical commitment and the long-standing arrangements for celebration of Mass in the Abbey; and, in relation to the Abbey itself, with the renewal of the Community's lease of the buildings due in 1999, the need to consolidate and preserve the increasingly close working relationship with the Cathedral Trustees and their management company, Iona Abbey Ltd, in a way that reflects the different concerns and perspectives but also the common interest in achieving a harmonious partnership.

There are many challenging issues concerning the future of the Community's islands work that are under consideration as we look to and plan for the years ahead. How can the ministry of hospitality and the experience of community best be offered in the face of the increasing demand? How can we ensure that our centres remain accessible to all, when the pressure is to book early but the evidence clearly points to the Iona experience being at its richest when there is a wide range of guests, often from different social and national backgrounds? (And this is a matter of culture — the way things are structured — as much as finance, since strenuous and successful attempts have been made to create a subsidy fund for those who might not otherwise be able to afford the costs. Indeed the Community was the subject of a case-study for a recent business studies textbook which questioned our reluctance to charge what the market will bear!) How do we continue to incarnate and convey the Community's 'story' and concerns through a group of staff among whom there may be very few Community Members and Associates? Is it now time to move away from the 'resident group' model of staffing and look at other possibilities? Is there some way of scaling down the pace and intensity of life in the centres, which is so demanding for staff week by week, so as to achieve a gentler culture and still provide a potentially fulfilling experience for guests? The questions are legion; perhaps it is when the Community stops asking them that the wing-beat of the Wild Goose will be out of earshot!

Over recent years there has been an increasing groundswell of opinion within the Community about the possible development of the mainland work. It has long been said that the main work of the Community is what Members do in their own local situations to express the Community's concerns through their own lives, and that the function of the Community's staff is to support and facilitate this process. To an extent this is still true. But the reality is also that for many years the Community has employed mainland staff on a range of corporate activities, most notably during the lifetime of Community House in Clyde Street until its closure in 1977. With the expansion of the Community's membership and the identification of additional areas of concern (three further ones relating to work and unemployment, sexuality issues, and inter-faith dialogue having been added in 1996 to those agreed earlier), questions have been raised about the need for a greater degree of co-ordination and for improved communication, so as to achieve a more effective focus and keep all informed of what is happening. There is clearly room for debate here about whether the cutting edge is at its sharpest when wielded on few or many fronts, and whether a controlled and centralized approach or a more flexible, inevitably uneven and looser process best reflects the ethos of the Community and is appropriate to the contemporary social, political and cultural realities.

There is also a growing feeling that a different kind of mainland base is needed — something more than the present administrative headquarters in which there is scarcely room for current requirements. So possibilities are being explored which might accommodate a sales outlet and provide opportunities for hospitality and relating more creatively to the local community than is feasible at the moment. The commitment to 'travel light' remains strong, however, among many Members, and there is still a vivid corporate recollection of past problems with buildings: here too, therefore, the discussions will be interesting and demanding!

Underpinning all the Community's life there has been an increasing awareness of the significance of 'spirituality' especially in today's society, described so often as post-Christian, post-modern, pluralistic. The rediscovery of spirituality was identified and agreed in the 1989 strategic planning process as one of the Community's areas of concern. What brings so many people to Iona is essentially a spiritual journey in search of meaning, purpose and value at a time when so many of the old certainties seem to be breaking down, exposed as inadequate to the tensions, questions and pressures of today, and traditional institutions, the Church included, do not fully meet people's needs. 'Celtic spirituality' in particular has a fascination, a curiosity value and attraction because of its perceived association with remote natural beauty and the past, and is often explored in the context of the quest for personal growth that reflects the current individualistic ethos. The Iona Community's understanding of spirituality, however, has to do with engagement rather than the kind of escape that smacks of nostalgia and the romantic. It is founded on the incarnational theology that has characterized the life of the Community since its outset. It asserts that the genuine Celtic tradition of spirituality, as found in the Columban church, had a strong social and communal dimension: God is thoroughly down-to-earth, to be discovered, encountered and experienced not only in personal reflective meditation but also in the practicalities and particularities of life, in human struggles and relationships as much as in tranquility and the contemplation of natural beauty. 'Spirituality is where prayer and politics meet', as Kate McIlhagga, a Community Member who is a United Reformed Church minister in the North of England, has said.

It is perhaps in this area, in continuing to assert that spirituality is about an energizing kind of connectedness, and in witnessing and embodying this integrated approach in all our concerns and activities, that the Community's main contribution to the renewal of the Church and society has been and will be made. Members of the Community such as John Bell of the Wild Goose Resource Group and Kathy Galloway, editor of the Community's bi-monthly magazine *Coracle*, as well as John Harvey, now working in Glasgow with the Craighead Institute of Faith and Life, receive more invitations than they can accept to talk and lead workshops throughout Britain and beyond on this and related themes. Consistently people say that what interests and attracts them about the Community is its attempt to discover new ways to express and explore the Christian faith so as to make it real and relevant to contemporary needs and experience, through worship, through affirming that an ecumenical approach is imperative, through holding spiritual and social concerns inextricably together as parts of a single reality.

There is little new in this. It has been the essence of the Community from the beginning. For almost sixty years now this has been the mainspring of all Community Members' commitment and the theme to which Leaders have returned in their writing, preaching and talking. It is instructive to see how often John Harvey, while Leader, emphasized, for example, the 'conviction that God is at work in the midst of life', the significance of discipline and obedience, the importance of seeking to discern 'God's purpose in events' (a phrase of Ralph Morton's) and 'Christ's place in today's society', and the Church's vocation as 'a community of subversive orthodoxy'.

The last ten years, as the last sixty, have had their ups and downs!

But they have never been other than interesting. Despite all the encouraging signs the Community remains ever-aware of its own frailty and fragility. We see no virtue in the Community's continuing existence unless we still have a job to do within the purpose and providence of God. Just as there have been changes in the past, so there will be changes in the future, as the context, the needs and the demands and indeed the character and composition of the Community, keep changing. We are conscious of our vulnerability both as individuals and as a movement and organization: we know we do not and probably shall not get it right all the time; but that is unavoidable if we strive to be faithful to the vision and values of the kingdom and maintain our precarious position on the edge of risk.

From time to time we are asked about the authenticity of the Wild Goose as a Celtic symbol of the Holy Spirit; and consultations with certain Celtic scholars have failed to allay the suspicion that the origins can be traced no further back than George MacLeod's imagination! But, as is amply borne out by the earlier chapters of this book and the collection of stories and allusions that have been accumulated over the years, it is a symbol that has all sorts of rich, creative and inspiring connotations and possibilities. John Harvey enjoyed recounting the experience of one of the Community's Members, in the United States for a year, who said, 'I was telling someone about the wild goose being a symbol of the Holy Spirit in the Celtic Church. He replied, 'Well, that wouldn't work in America because here the wild goose is a pest and people shoot it.' I didn't think it at the time, but I realized that if ever there was a good reason for the wild goose being a symbol of the Holy Spirit it was because it is a pest and people want to shoot it!'

The chase and the challenge go on!

Norman Shanks
June 1997

Selected Bibliography

Anderson, A. O. and M. O., *Adomnan's Life of Columba* (Nelson & Sons 1961)

Bede, *A History of the English Church and People* (Penguin, London 1974)

Bell, John and Maule, Graham, *Songs of the Incarnation* (Iona Community, Wild Goose Publications, Glasgow 1985)

Bell, John and Maule, Graham, Wild Goose Songs Vol 1, *Heaven Shall Not Wait* (Iona Community, Wild Goose Publications, Glasgow 1989)

Bell, John and Maule, Graham, Wild Goose Songs Vol 2, *Enemy of Apathy* (Iona Community, Wild Goose Publications, Glasgow 1988)

Bell, John and Maule, Graham, Wild Goose Songs Vol 3, *Love From Below* (Iona Community, Wild Goose Publications, Glasgow 1989)

Bradley, Ian, *The Celtic Way* (Darton, Longman and Todd, London 1993)

Bradley, Ian, *Columba, Pilgrim and Penitent* (Wild Goose Publications, Glasgow 1996)

Bulloch, James, *The Life of the Celtic Church* (Saint Andrew Press, Edinburgh 1963)

Bunting, Mitchell, *Columba: The Man and the Myth* (Iona Community, Wild Goose Publications, Glasgow 1986)

Chadwick, Nora, *The Age of the Saints in the Early Celtic Church* (Oxford University Press 1961)

Colin Baxter Island Guides - Iona (Colin Baxter, Grantown-on-Spey 1997)

Ferguson, Ron, *Daily Readings with George MacLeod* (HarperCollins, London 1991)

Ferguson, Ron, *Geoff: The Life of Geoffrey M. Shaw* (Famedram, 1979)

Ferguson, Ron, *George MacLeod* (HarperCollins, London 1990)

Ferguson, Ron, *Grace and Dysentery* (Iona Community, Wild Goose Publications, Glasgow 1987)

Finlay, Ian, *Columba* (Victor Gollancz, London 1979)

Hale, R. B., *The Magnificent Gael* (World Media Publications, Canada 1986)

Harvey, John, *Bridging the Gap: Has the Church Failed the Poor?* (Saint Andrew Press, Edinburgh 1987)

MacArthur, E. Mairi, *Columba's Island* (University Press, Edinburgh 1995)

MacArthur, E. Mairi, *Iona, The Living Memory of a Crofting Community, 1750-1914* (University Press, Edinburgh 1990)

MacLeod, George F., *We Shall Rebuild* (Iona Community 1944 and 1962)

MacLeod, George F., *Only One Way Left* (Iona Community 1956)

MacLeod, George F., *The Whole Earth Shall Cry Glory: Iona Prayers by Revd George F. MacLeod* (Iona Community, Wild Goose Publications, Glasgow 1985)

McNeill, Marian F., *An Iona Anthology* (Iona Community 1952)

McNeill, John T., *The Celtic Churches* (University of Chicago Press 1974)

MacQuarrie, Alan, *Iona Through the Ages* (Society of Highland and Island Historical Research 1983)

Menzies, Lucy, *St Columba of Iona* (J. M Dent, London 1970)

Murray, Ellen, *Peace and Adventure* (Iona Community 1947 and 1987)

Morton, Ralph, *The Household of Faith* (Iona Community 1951)

Morton, Ralph, *The Twelve Together* (Iona Community 1956)

Morton, Ralph, *The Iona Community: Personal Impressions of the Early Years* (Saint Andrew Press, Edinburgh 1974)

Tillich, Paul, *The Courage To Be* (Collins 1962)

The Iona Community is:

- An ecumenical movement of men and women from different walks of life and different traditions in the Christian church
- Committed to the gospel of Jesus Christ, and to following where that leads, even into the unknown
- Engaged together, and with people of goodwill across the world, in acting, reflecting and praying for justice, peace and the integrity of creation
- Convinced that the inclusive community we seek must be embodied in the community we practise

Together with our staff, we are responsible for:

- Our islands residential centres of Iona Abbey, the MacLeod Centre on Iona, and Camas Adventure Centre on the Ross of Mull

and in Glasgow:

- The administration of the Community
- Our work with young people
- Our publishing house, Wild Goose Publications
- Our association in the revitalising of worship with the Wild Goose Resource Group

The Iona Community was founded in Glasgow in 1938 by George MacLeod, minister, visionary and prophetic witness for peace, in the context of the poverty and despair of the Depression. Its original task of rebuilding the monastic ruins of Iona Abbey became a sign of hopeful rebuilding of community in Scotland and beyond. Today, we are about 250 Members, mostly in Britain, and 1500 Associate Members, with 1400 Friends worldwide. Together and apart, 'we follow the light we have, and pray for more light'.

For information on the Iona Community contact: The Iona Community, Fourth Floor, Savoy House, 140 Sauchiehall Street, Glasgow G2 3DH, UK. Phone: 0141 332 6343
e-mail: ionacomm@gla.iona.org.uk; web: www.iona.org.uk

For enquiries about visiting Iona, please contact: Iona Abbey, Isle of Iona, Argyll PA76 6SN, UK. Phone: 01681 700404
e-mail: ionacomm@iona.org.uk

CPSIA information can be obtained at www.ICGtesting.com
Printed in the USA
LVOW11s1932261214

420500LV00001B/115/A